The Ultimate Gardener's Guide to Organic Weed Control

WEED

The Ultimate Gardener's Guide to Organic Weed Control

WEED

Tim Marshall

ABC
Books

The ABC 'Wave' device is a trademark of the Australian Broadcasting Corporation and is used under licence by HarperCollins*Publishers*Australia.

First published in Australia in 2010
by HarperCollins*Publishers*Australia Pty Limited
ABN 36 009 913 517
harpercollins.com.au

Copyright © Text Tim Marshall 2010
The right of Tim Marshall to be identified as the author of this work
has been asserted by him in accordance with the *Copyright
Amendment (Moral Rights) Act 2000.*

This work is copyright. Apart from any use as permitted under the
Copyright Act 1968, no part may be reproduced, copied, scanned,
stored in a retrieval system, recorded, or transmitted, in any form
or by any means, without the prior written permission of the publisher.

HarperCollins*Publishers*
Level 13, 201 Elizabeth Street, Sydney NSW 2000, Australia
Unit D, 63 Apollo Drive, Rosedale, Auckland 0632, New Zealand
A 53, Sector 57, Noida, UP, India
1 London Bridge Street, London SE1 9GF, United Kingdom
2 Bloor Street East, 20th floor, Toronto, Ontario M4W 1A8, Canada
195 Broadway, New York NY 10007, USA

National Library of Australia Cataloguing-in-Publication data:

Marshall, Tim.
  Weed: the ultimate gardener's guide to organic weed control / Tim Marshall.
  ISBN 978 0 7333 2774 2 (pbk.)
  Includes index.
  Weeds–Control. Weeds.
  Australian Broadcasting Corporation.
632.5

Cover design by Priscilla Nielsen
Internal design by Jane Waterhouse
Illustrations by Ian Faulkner
Cover image by Kurtwilson/Getty Images; all other images by shutterstock.com
Index by IndexAT
Typeset in Minion Pro 10.5/14pt by Letter Spaced

Many people have contributed to this book and to my knowledge of weeds. A few of them have received a special mention in the acknowledgments, but it is not possible to thank them all.

Two people deserve an extra acknowledgment for their support and assistance.

Thanks to Andre Leu for his tireless work for the organic industry, as the Chairperson of the Organic Federation of Australia and Vice President of the International Federation of Organic Agriculture Movements, as an exemplary organic tropical fruit producer, skilled plants-man and prolific plant-hunter, trainer and writer, supportive colleague to many and a valued friend and adviser to me.

My partner, Dr Anne-Marie Morgan, has provided much support and encouragement to me during the preparation of this book, despite her own busy life and obligations to family, work and her own publishing schedule.

FOREWORD

At last — the book that we have all been waiting for!

Tim Marshall has been a leader in the organic movement since the '70s and is regarded as one of Australia's top organic experts. His work has focused primarily on commercial growers and was not readily available for home gardeners, until now. Practical and jam-packed with Tim's insights — gained from years of personal experience dealing with a whole range of garden, agricultural and horticultural weeds — *Weed* makes his knowledge readily available for us to utilise. It is easy to read, highly informative and convincing, especially on the pressing need for all gardeners to adopt an organic approach.

Very few gardeners find fun in weeding. It is a chore for most of us, and for those of us trying to garden without using chemicals it can be overwhelming. This book provides the information on how to deal successfully with the weeds in our gardens or small land holdings. This could be to eradicate them completely or maybe to understand that they actually serve a useful purpose. As Emerson said, a weed is simply 'a plant whose virtues have not yet been discovered'.

In this book Tim teaches us to understand the weeds, how they multiply and how they compete, how to read them as a reflection of soil condition, and how to use this understanding to exploit their weaknesses — and covers many other topics. There is a list of common garden weeds and suggestions on how to deal with them easily and effectively without the use of chemicals. Importantly, Tim provides reassurance that although many weeds will take a great deal of persistence and effort to control, it is possible and that it will eventually work.

They say that knowledge is power, and with the knowledge gained from this book, I am sure you too will feel inspired to claim victory over the weeds in your garden.

So, *Weed: The Ultimate Gardener's Guide to Organic Weed Control* follows on perfectly from Tim's recent book *Bug: The Ultimate Gardener's Guide to Organic Pest Control*, and his previous publication *Composting: The Ultimate Organic Gardener's Guide to Recycling Your Garden*. These are all essential garden tools for all gardeners.

Sophie Thomson
Gardening writer, *Gardening Australia magazine*

INTRODUCTION

GO ORGANIC OR STAY WITH CHEMICALS?

Whether (or to what extent) anyone adopts organic practices in their garden or on their farm is entirely their choice. We hope this book helps readers see the potential for organic management on their property. We hope too that all chemical users stay within the law and consider the human and environmental consequences of what they are doing. Most people will try to be careful these days; most people want to get it right and will avoid chemicals where they can. Unfortunately, in the many years I spent in professional land management positions and as a resident of a rural district I have seen some careless mistakes and some unintended errors caused by bad advice, or simply a lack of information or not following label instructions. In the recent past it was common for users of agricultural chemicals to have simply failed to understand that chemicals can produce chronic damage. Because they suffered no acute pain, or pain that was only short-lived, they did not take adequate precautions. In the days before a certificate was needed to purchase very dangerous S7 chemicals, many users were unaware that 'a little more for good luck' inevitably hastened resistance, did more environmental harm, was probably no more cost-effective and may have been economically more costly and, most importantly, was much worse for their personal exposure.

Over the past two decades the development of Integrated Pest Management and biological control programs, as well as the increasing awareness of the toxicity of insecticides, have encouraged more growers to adopt organic or low-chemical-input pest control. Herbicides have proven harder to abandon. We are not as aware of the negative side effects of herbicides, widespread access to biological control is not simple or straightforward, and the fear of weeds is deeply woven into our minds.

Also unfortunate is the paucity of really good information about how to use organic principles, especially on larger acreages. In a climate-change-aware world, we now understand better the need for urgent action to reduce our carbon footprint. What better technology to adopt than organic principles, which are precisely about improving the soil ecosystem, with the inevitable and beneficial outcome of storing more carbon. Soil is the largest accessible storage place for carbon and our entire system of food production should run completely on the sun, with just a few natural inputs. If it did, we could store much of the carbon production of the Western world in our soil. When we increase the carbon content of soil with humus, virtually every measurable characteristic of the soil improves and the food we produce becomes more nutritious and beneficial for our health.

The main reason more people don't take up organic growing practices is a lack of access to good information. The organic philosophy was misunderstood and ignored for too long by agricultural researchers and trainers, and many ecologically sound traditional practices were almost lost as agriculture became increasingly industrialised. But there is hope. An excellent example of a traditional practice revitalised is the under-vine management strategy adopted by forward-thinking organic viticulturists in the McLaren Vale district, where they use soursob as a cover crop underneath their vines. Using advanced irrigation monitoring systems and superior plough design they are able to limit soursob growth to the narrow strip directly under the canopy where this useful winter cover crop dies down naturally to form mulch over the summer. It doesn't grow through the main growing period of the vines and therefore doesn't compete for water.

A traditional definition of a weed is 'a plant growing where it is not wanted' but these growers have taken a commonly agreed 'weed' — soursob — and have applied an organic management system that reclassifies it as a 'useful' and an integral component of vineyard operation. Knowledge is the key to their success — and knowledge comes free. The growers have significantly reduced their carbon footprint and eliminated toxic chemicals in the process. Their knowledge was backed up by practical application and observation. Tools and equipment were researched, trialled, modified (or abandoned if necessary), but they have ended up with a practical system that almost entirely eliminates weed contamination and water competition. The number of passes they make with a tractor is comparable to a non-organic vineyard, and the energy in the herbicides and pesticides they avoid drops their overall energy consumption by as much as 30 per cent.

Organic growing is not just about a list of chemicals to avoid, nor should it really be about a list of alternative treatments for things. To really adopt an organic frame of mind is to recognise that it's always best to work with nature. Anything else should be considered as a stopgap measure. Instead, chemicals have become a convenient crutch.

The rise of Integrated Weed Management is the result of concern about the environment. More emphasis is now put on alternative and natural methods of weed control, including cultivation, mowing and mulching.

One area of disagreement persists between the integrated and the organic land managers. It concerns the effects of herbicides on soil biology. Herbicide advocates have tended to dismiss herbicide activity in the soil as relatively benign. Recent research, however, supports the position that the organic community has always maintained — herbicide residues inhibit the development of a flourishing diversity of soil organisms. In particular, herbicides, together with nitrogenous fertilisers, severely limit biological nitrogen fixation, both from rhizobium bacteria in legumes and especially the activity of free-living 'nitrogen-fixers' such as azotobacter and cyanobacteria.

This book provides basic information on organic weed control for the home gardener or small landowner. There are very few other sources of information specifically on organic methods. To apply organic methods efficiently and well, gardeners should also be prepared to rely on their own ability to observe and assess for themselves the appropriateness of the suggested methods to their own site, depending upon the particular weeds present and their extent, and their own physical and time limitations.

Significant persistence is sometimes required to eradicate weeds using organic methods. Repeated visits are often needed to pull or dig weeds and to attend to mulch cover and the growth of green manures and cover crops. The suggestions made throughout this book are based on three major strategies that will help your organic control program become a success. They are:

- **Stop** weeds from producing **seeds** and other propagating parts. Use dead-heading, mowing and grazing to reduce or eliminate seed production whenever possible.
- **Regular** and **consistent** attention is better than spasmodic every time — even if you have only a little time, try to make regular daily or weekly periods available to follow up your work.
- **Work** from an **edge**, starting with the area of least weed incidence and moving into the main area of infestation. Keep the work zone within the limits of what you can achieve and don't move to the next area until the first area is clean.

ACKNOWLEDGMENTS

Many gardeners, farmers and researchers have contributed to my knowledge and experience of organic weed control, but special mention should be made of Dave Duncan and Stephanie Goldfinch, both experts in weed identification and control. They read an early draft of this book and made useful comments, as did Doug Bickerton.

Thanks also to Joch Boshworth, Maurice Franklin, Lex Langridge, Andre Leu, Rod May, Michael Plane, Jonathan Sturm, Adam Voysey and Joyce Wilkie for sharing their organic knowledge, experience and good companionship over many years.

Andy Nicholls and I did not always agree on the viability of organic weed control techniques or the need for herbicide use; however, we always agreed on the requirement for proper training and appropriate caution when using herbicides. Andy and I learnt something about weed management from each other and have developed an enduring respect and friendship despite our sometimes different views.

CONTENTS

Foreword *Sophie Thomson* vii

Introduction ix

Acknowledgments xiii

How to use this book xvi

What is a weed? 1

Take control 42

Garden weeds 144

Good weeds 165

Environmental weeds 180

Weed control quick reference 193

Glossary and resources 210

Case study: Tim's garden 218

Index 224

HOW TO USE THIS BOOK

Firstly, this is not a weed identification book. There are good handbooks available from bookshops, garden centres, departments of agriculture and environment, water catchment boards, local government and the internet. See Chapter 7 for a list of resource books and websites. Instead, this book will help you learn about the wide range of effective and easy non-chemical control methods available to gardeners and landholders. It will also assist in your understanding of the ecological role of weeds, including why they establish, how they compete and how their particular weaknesses can be exploited in a control program.

Use this book to stimulate your observation skills and to reconsider which weeds should be receiving priority treatment. You will always have weeds, but you can influence which weeds you have. Are there some weeds that you can you control with simple tools, are not too unsightly, or have some positive attributes? More importantly perhaps, use this book to reinvigorate your enthusiasm for organic methods and strengthen your determination to avoid toxic and ecologically disruptive synthetic herbicides. Organic control is not always easy, but it is possible and sometimes more cost-effective then chemical control.

Knowledge, observation and consistency are the key tools available to organic growers. I hope this book improves your stock of each.

1
What is a weed?

There is no scientific or botanical definition for 'weed' as such. A commonly used description might be 'a plant growing out of place' or 'a plant growing where it is not wanted', but this is not really a botanical definition.

Even those plants that we refer to in common parlance as 'weeds' have a place where they are native and 'belong' as part of the natural ecosystem. Many weeds found in gardens and cropping land in southern Australia are from South Africa: plants such as soursob (*Oxalis pes-caprae*), Cape tulip (*Homeria* species), Cape lily (*Ornithogalum thyrsoides*) and African daisy (*Senecio pterophorus*). Several species of Australian eucalypts have, in turn, become weeds in South Africa, Portugal, Nepal, California and elsewhere. Some plants are considered weeds in certain areas, for instance *Echium plantagineum*, known as Paterson's curse in the Eastern states, but as salvation Jane in South Australia — where it was sometimes welcome fodder for sheep in times of drought as well as being a valuable food source for bees. In recent times, we would say good pasture management provides much better feed value than salvation Jane so we should eliminate it, but the example of two different views of the same plant is still interesting.

Even more curiously, plants such as ryegrass (*Lolium* species) may be a major economic plus in one year as the basis of the pasture phase, but a major economic weed in another part of the rotation when cereal crops are grown. In the home garden, couch grass (*Agropyron repens*) is the basis of the home lawn and is coddled with more irrigation, fertiliser and pesticide than any agricultural crop. But couch is a major weed centimetres away in the border plantings or in the flower garden. In a bowling green or a neatly manicured formal lawn, plants such as the lawn daisy (*Bellis perennis*) may be unthinkable, but in my lawn it would be welcome as a splash of colour, habitat for beneficial insects and a healthy indication of diversity (they also grow well even when mown and without needing fertiliser or pesticide).

So potentially, any plant may be a weed. Weeds may also have many valuable uses. They may be useful medicinal or culinary herbs, provide habitat for animals, birds and insects, and their roots may encourage soil fauna or flora. They may be attractive to look at as well as helping to bind, protect and build soil where the original flora has been lost.

G. H. Clarke, writing in the *Journal of the Australian Institute of Agricultural Science* in 1937, said the word 'weed' exemplifies our preference for nouns rather than verbs. The word probably originated as a corruption of *weod*, the Anglo-Saxon word for woad or dyeweed (*Isatis tinctoria*) and the first record of its use is from Aelfred (Alfred the Great) in about 888 CE. Woad would not be considered a weed in modern agriculture or gardening, and its growth habit is not typical of problem weeds. However, it does easily emerge from disturbed soil and may have troubled early agriculturists with a much smaller suite of tools at hand. The 'tares' of the New Testament, liberally translated as 'weeds', are generally agreed to be darnel (*Lolium temulentum*), still a major problem in grain crops in Europe. Other languages tend to be more descriptive, using the word for 'herb' plus an adjective — *mauvaise herbe* in French, *erbaccia* in Italian and *unkraut* in German.

Ecologists sought a better definition of the concept in the mid-'70s when their discipline came to prominence in agricultural affairs. Their better, yet still unsatisfactory, definitions are represented by the following quotation, from CSIRO scientist Milton Moore, also writing in the *Journal of the Australian Institute of Agricultural Science* in 1975: 'A plant is only a weed where it interferes with man's use of the land for particular purposes, with his well-being or with the quality of the environment.'

For our purposes, a weed is only a weed when it interferes with human activity — and that therefore makes every species and every individual plant potentially a weed. We do, however, commonly label certain species of plant as a weed, wherever and whenever it is growing, and we sometimes attach to that word a legal connotation that requires us to take particular actions or precautions.

WEEDS IN HISTORY

In European agricultural history, weeds were thought to just spring from the ground. They were regarded as the work of the devil, in fact. In this tradition, the ground had been cursed after the fall of Adam and Eve and thistles were sent as punishment: 'Cursed is the ground because of you, in toil you shall eat of it all the days of your life; thorns and thistles it shall bring forth to you; in the sweat of your face you shall eat bread'; Genesis 3: 18–19.

Francis Bacon and John Donne both thought that bad seed 'turned into' weeds. Donne writes, 'Good seed degenerates and oft obeys the soil's disease, and into Cockle strays', and Bacon echoes this in 1625 with, 'Another disease is the putting forth of wild oats, whereinto corn oftentimes (especially barley) doth degenerate. It happeneth chiefly from the weakness of the grain that is sown; for if it be too old or mouldy, it will bring forth wild oats.'

These ideas had been around for quite a while. In 300 BCE, the Greek philosopher and botanical writer Theophrastus believed that barley changed to weeds after heavy rains. In 1703, the Dutch artist

Romeyn de Hooghe wrote: 'While man is dreaming sinners' dreams, the weeds enjoy their growth.'

During the 17th and 18th centuries, it was common to associate weeds with sin and the devil, and to use charms and spells against weeds. Sir Thomas Browne (1605–82) observed Norfolk farmers placing chalked tiles inscribed with protective symbols at the corner and middle of fields to protect against dodder and common celandine.

Jethro Tull — a moniker that may be familiar to some as a popular rock band of the '60s and '70s — was an 18th-century agriculturalist who believed his system of agriculture would eliminate weeds altogether. In *Horse-Hoeing Husbandry* (printed in 1751) he wrote, 'All experienced husbandmen ... would unanimously agree to extirpate their whole race as entirely as in England they have done the wolves, though much more innocent and less rapacious than weeds.' He also called them a 'savage, wicked brood'. Tull is a significant player in the development of modern agriculture because he was the first person to pull a multi-row implement behind a horse. Cultivation and sowing tools had been attached to animals or humans before, but only as single-row tools. Tull thought his ideas would put an end to weeds as a serious problem of agriculture. Needless to say, Tull's horse-drawn hoe did not eliminate weeds, even though it was a dramatic innovation. Tull also advocated crop rotation.

WEEDS IN LANGUAGE AND LITERATURE

There are many literary and language references to weeds. We talk about growing 'rank and weedy' for instance and our language is subtly influenced by our attitude to weeds and vice versa.

Shakespeare's *Hamlet*, Act I, Scene II, contains the lines:

> *How weary, stale, flat and unprofitable*
> *Seem to me all the uses of this world!*

*Fie on't! O Fie! 'Tis an unweeded garden
That grows to seed.*

In *Henry V*, Act V, Scene II, we read:

*And all her husbandry doth lie in heaps
Corrupting in its own fertility.
... her fallow leas
The darnel, hemlock and rank fumitory,
Doth root upon, while the coulter rusts
That should deracinate such savagery;
The even mead ...
Wanting the scythe, all uncorrected, rank,
Conceives by idleness and nothing teems
But hateful docks, rough thistles, kecksies, burrs,
Losing both beauty and utility.*

The great British horticulturist, botanist and writer Anthony Huxley refers to weeds as 'These vegetable free-booters ...' and as 'carpetbaggers' in his book *Plant and Planet*, published in 1987.

The influence of this 'cultural baggage', reinforced through rich linguistic associations, is carried into our agricultural and horticultural operations and home gardens. The way in which humans have thought and written about weeds over the centuries still influences our understanding in modern times. Prejudice is inculcated into our activities to a large extent, and we take many things for granted because of it. If we wish to approach the issue of weeds from an ecological perspective and try to understand more holistically how and why human activity produced the phenomenon of weeds, we should first learn to question some of the assumptions implicit in these everyday references to weeds.

The story of Jethro Tull

Jethro Tull was an inventor of agricultural machinery and one of the founders of our modern system of agriculture.

Before Tull's invention became available, farmers walked up and down their fields broadcasting seed by hand. Not only did this method give an uneven distribution, it was wasteful of seed and sowers had to carry heavy bags of seed around with them.

Tull's first major agricultural invention was the multi-row mechanical seed drill in 1701. Pulled behind a horse, it consisted of a wheeled buggy with a seed box and a wheel-driven ratchet that evenly distributed the seed.

The seed drill was a major advance not only because it planted seeds at regular intervals but also at the right depth and then covered them with earth. This saved seed and ensured the seed was sown in straight lines — handy for Tull to also invent a horse-drawn hoe. With the advent of these innovations, mechanised agriculture could really start to develop.

Tull was not just a tinkerer with machines — he was a thinker and a visionary agriculturist. He advocated pulverising or crumbling soil so that air and moisture could penetrate to the roots of plants. He also stressed the importance of manure and promoted the use of horses instead of oxen.

Tull wrote *Horse-Hoeing Husbandry* in 1731 to persuade English and European farmers to adopt his technology. Other inventors improved his seed drill design by adding gears to the seed spreader in 1782, but the fundamental concept and mechanism of Tull's seed drill is still evident in modern sowing technology.

> Tull and some other agriculturists founded the Norfolk system, which advocated a scientific approach to crop rotation. The Norfolk system incorporated the mechanised farming invented by Tull and used a four-part rotation system rather than three. The group also introduced many new crops to England and promoted a scientific understanding of the principles of stock breeding, with the effect of significantly improving the productivity of animal farming. The rotation system planted wheat in the first year, turnips (winter stockfeed) in the second, barley with clover undersown in year three, and in the last year ryegrass was added to the clover and the field was grazed. This system was highly productive and removed the need for a traditional fallow year.

INTRODUCTION OF WEEDS INTO AUSTRALIA

A significant percentage of weed species are introduced plants. Some are escapees from agriculture or ornamental gardening and some are accidental introductions.

Early colonial records do not discuss weeds in any great depth. Botanist Robert Brown prepared the first list of weeds in the colony of New South Wales in 1802. It contained 25 species. Most of the early weeds listed in all the colonies were European in origin — not surprisingly, as most early settlers struggled to produce a landscape that mirrored the familiar patterns of their homelands, including garden plants that became weedy in the new country. However, there are also examples of weeds that originate from ports of call on the journey between Britain and Australia, including Brazil (prickly pear *Opuntia* species and *Lantana camara*) and South Africa (soursob *Oxalis pes-caprae*).

The attempt to 'Europeanise' the colonies was formalised by the so-called Acclimatisation Societies, especially during the period

1860 to 1890. They advocated introduction of a wide range of plants and many of them became noxious weeds. Sir Ferdinand von Mueller, the first government botanist in Victoria, promoted 10 species that later became declared weeds in that state. He also gave seeds to Burke and Wills and encouraged them to plant some wherever they made camp. Indeed, when Dr Richard Schomburgh, the director of the Botanic Gardens in Adelaide, wrote Australia's first monograph on weeds in 1878, it was widely ignored and hardly reported or reviewed.

Renowned weed scientist Dr Peter Kloot has made some excellent reviews of weeds in early South Australian records. He lists 90 introductions between 1847 and 1852, or 15 species per year on average. The average rate of weed introductions for 1836 to 1984 is 6.1 species per year, for a total of 904 alien plants, of which 57 per cent are apparently unintentional introductions and 43 per cent are intentional. In other words, 10 per cent of plants introduced in this period became weeds.

CAN NATIVE PLANTS BE WEEDS?

The term 'native' refers to the place or country in which a plant originated and 'indigenous' means native to the local area as defined by a particular soil type or other biological and geographical regional boundaries. Native plants may be indigenous to a particular Australian habitat, but when they escape from that habitat and become invasive in another area they may certainly be regarded as weeds. The line at which a plant stops being indigenous and starts being a weed can also be difficult to define. Hardline indigenous vegetation buffs may never want to see a plant considered weedy when it remains within the area to which it is indigenous, but others will have no problem conceptualising a plant as weedy if it is 'where it is not wanted'. In fact, most plants do not behave like weeds within their native range. This is partly because species in their native range are usually limited by particular diseases or eaten by herbivores only found in that range. These limiting factors are usually not introduced to the new environment at the same time that the plant becomes weedy. With some exceptions, most plants both compete with and share their native habitat with other plant and animal species, limiting and controlling the abundance of each other.

Sweet pittosporum (*Pittosporum undulatum*) is an example of a native tree that has become seriously weedy in the Adelaide Hills and in Southeast Queensland, well beyond its pre-European range. Like some other natives that have become weeds, it is often planted as an ornamental tree. Birds and animals easily disperse the fruit, and changed fire regimes have assisted its survival in areas previously infrequently burnt but now subject to regular fire.

Other Australian native plants that have become weedy include numerous wattles such as Cootamundra wattle (*Acacia baileyana*), coastal wattle (*A. sophorae*) and golden wreath (*A. saligna)*, coast tea tree (*Leptospermum laevigatum*), burgan (*Kunzea ericoides*) and bluebell creeper (*Billardiera heterophylla*, formerly *Sollya heterophylla*). Some natives such as acacias and *Grevillea rosmarinifolia* readily hybridise with local indigenous plants, thereby threatening the genetic identity of indigenous species.

THE ECONOMIC IMPACT OF WEEDS

Invasive weeds are a serious threat to agriculture and to the Australian natural environment. They cause damage to natural landscapes, agricultural land, waterways and coastal areas.

There are about 3,000 plants commonly recognised and classified as weeds in Australia, meaning that they have established self-supporting populations and cause harm to agriculture, people or the natural environment.

A Geographic Atlas of World Weeds by Le Roy Holm et al. (John Wiley and Sons, New York, 1979) lists some 8,000 species of weeds from over a quarter of a million species of flowering plants and ferns known at the time. Of these, less than 1,000 have become a serious problem on a world scale.

Estimates of losses caused to agriculture and society in general by weeds are notoriously hard to make and conflicting statements and estimates are easily found. All estimates agree, however, that losses caused by weeds are significant when compared with other pest problems and represent the greater percentage of total loss.

Australian government estimates of the impact of weeds is nearly $4 billion per year in reduced farm incomes and higher food costs and about $120 million of government funds spent each year on the cost of monitoring, controlling, management and research on weeds. This does not include the loss of environmental services, impact of weeds on human health or the unpaid labour of homeowners and community volunteers spent controlling weeds.

Because of gathering negative publicity since the publication of *Silent Spring* by Rachel Carson in 1962, figures for the total size of the chemical industry are hard to find and not well publicised. However, according to the United States Environmental Protection Authority a reasonable estimate of the global sales of herbicides would be USD$14,500 billion per annum, about 44 per cent of the total pesticide expenditure, and that does not include the cost of applying them.

A strictly economic assessment of the effect of weeds on crops or other activities, as well as the cost of control, may also reveal that much effort will not be rewarded. For instance, brassica can be quite sensitive to weed competition when the plants are small, but by the third trimester of growth when the maturing plants occupy the space well, weed control operations will rarely be worthwhile in terms of increased yield. A limited amount of roguing (removing the seed heads) of weeds may be justified in order to reduce the seed burden for subsequent crops. However, many growers feel uncomfortable with untidy-looking crops and pour effort into control because of their preference for a tidy-looking field rather than on the basis of sound economic information. Very little garden weed control could be said to be strictly 'economically rational'.

WEED LEGISLATION

Weed legislation in Australia originally focussed on eradication, following on from Tull's concept to deracinate (meaning: *pull out by the roots*) them entirely. However, it is rarely possible to eradicate weeds. We can only really eradicate them when we are dealing with small or limited outbreaks of recently introduced weeds. Legislative and regulatory approaches are now focussed on control. More recently, enlightened practitioners have adopted the approach of prevention.

Each state has a system of declared or proclaimed weeds. Depending on the level or class of proclamation, landowners may be obligated to control them to limit their spread or to eradicate them. Proclaimed weeds and landowner requirements vary but a web guide to each state's legislation can be found at http://www.weeds.gov.au/government/roles/state.html. In some states, local government has a significant role in weed management. For example, the following classes apply in New South Wales:

- Class 1 — State prohibited weeds
  'Plants that pose a potentially serious threat to primary production or the environment and are not present in the State or are present only to a limited extent.'

  The intent is to provide a high level of action to those weeds of statewide significance.

- Class 2 — Regionally prohibited weeds
  'Plants that pose a potentially serious threat to primary production or the environment of a region to which the order applies and are not present in the region or are present to a limited extent.'

  The intent of this category is to provide a high level of control on a regional basis.

- Class 3 — Regionally controlled weeds
  'Plants that pose a serious threat to primary production or the environment of an area to which the order applies,

are not widely distributed in the area and are likely to spread in the area or to another area.'

This class is intended to provide for enforceable control, where necessary, on a local or regional basis.

- Class 4 — Locally controlled weeds
'Plants that pose the threat to primary production, the environment or human health, are widely distributed in an area to which the order applies and are likely to spread in the area or to another area.'

This class is intended to include common and widespread species as well as environmental weeds of more locally specific impact.

At the federal level, the Australian government's responsibility for quarantine is established in the *Quarantine Act 1908*, to prevent the introduction of weeds into Australia. The federal *Biological Control Act 1985* provides for a weed to be declared a target for biological control.

The *Environment Protection and Biodiversity Conservation Act 1999* also confers some responsibilities and powers.

Weeds of National Significance (WONS)

The list of 20 Weeds of National Significance (WONS) was developed using key criteria that investigated the following:

- invasive tendencies
- impacts
- potential for spread
- socio-economic and environmental values.

Under the National Weeds Strategy of 1998 (www.weeds.gov.au/publications/strategies/pubs/weed-strategy.pdf), Australian governments endorsed a framework to identify which weed species could be considered Weeds of National Significance within an agricultural, forestry and environmental context.

States and territories nominated 71 weed species to be assessed and ranked using four major criteria mentioned previously. Twenty WONS were identified through this process and national management strategies have been developed for all.

Managing WONS

Individual landowners and managers are ultimately responsible for managing WONS. State and territory governments are responsible for overall legislation and administration.

THE ECOLOGICAL PERSPECTIVE

The ecological interactions of weeds with crops may be positive, negative or benign. Negative interactions not only involve competition for water, nutrient or light; some weeds also compete against crops for pollinators by providing an easier access or more nectar per visit, and they subsequently reduce seed set for native, crop or garden plants.

Many weeds can harbour diseases or crops pests. Thistles, for instance, may host lettuce necrotic yellows virus, and cruciferous weeds such as

LIST OF WONS

- Prickly acacia (*Acacia nilotica*)
- Alligator weed (*Alternanthera philoxeroides*)
- Pond apple (*Annona glabra*)
- Bridal creeper (*Asparagus asparagoides*)
- Cabomba (*Cabomba caroliniana*)
- Boneseed, also called Bitou bush (*Chrysanthemoides monilifera*)
- Rubber vine (*Cryptostegia grandiflora*)
- Hymenachne (*Hymenachne amplexicaulis*)
- Lantana (*Lantana camara*)
- Mimosa (*Mimosa pigra*)
- Chilean needle grass (*Nassella neesiana*)
- Serrated tussock (*Nassella trichotoma*)
- Parkinsonia (*Parkinsonia aculeata*)
- Parthenium (*Parthenium hysterophorus*)
- Mesquite (*Prosopis* species)
- Blackberry (*Rubus fruticosus*)
- Willow (*Salix* species **except** *S.babylonica*, *S.x calodendron* and *S.x reichardtii*)
- Salvinia (*Salvinia molesta*)
- Athel pine (*Tamarix aphylla*)
- Gorse (*Ulex europaeus*)

wild radish (*Raphanus raphanistrum*), charlock (*Sinapis arvensis*) and turnip weed (*Rapistrum rugosum*) may host clubroot.

A problem with some weeds is that they are toxic to livestock. Salvation Jane may be acceptable sheep fodder, but it contains an alkaloid poisonous to horses. St John's wort (*Hypericum perforatum*) contains hypericin, a chemical that causes skin with light pigmentation to become sensitive to sunlight, as well as causing problems for cattle and other stock. Wild garlic is not toxic but will taint cow's milk within 5 to 6 minutes of ingestion.

Burrs in wool cause problems for producers; red-legged earth mite is harboured on the South African capeweed (*Arctotheca calendula*) and water hyacinth (*Eichhornia crassipes*) can block irrigation channels.

Park supervisors, local government and home gardeners spend tens of thousands of hours controlling them every month.

Although the negative effects of weeds are well known and recognised, there are also significant beneficial effects. Some weeds are important for interim soil stabilisation and protection where original vegetation has been lost. The economic contribution of weeds towards soil conservation has not been measured but must be large. Herbs such as chicory (*Cichorium* species), pennyroyal (*Mentha pulegium*), ribwort (*Plantago* species) and others are included in organic pastures for their beneficial function for animal health because they contain health-promoting chemicals. They also tend to have longer or seasonally different growing and dormancy cycles than traditional pasture plants, ensuring that plant enzymes and nutrient storage are optimal at times of the year when normal pasture species are less valuable. They may also have a role in sourcing nutrients from deeper in the soil profile, and may produce flowers with nectar and pollen food for beneficial wasps.

The species of weeds growing may provide an indication of soil fertility or condition. Docks (*Rumex* species) are often associated with wet or acid soils. Fat hen (*Chenopodium album*) is often associated with elevated nitrogen levels (the old chook pen), and tobacco tree (*Nicotiana glauca*), an Argentinean import, grows strongly in copper-rich soils. In any neglected or unoccupied site, nature will produce plants to fill the ecological niche. The question here is, why this particular species? What advantage does this species have and what soil (edaphic) or other ecological conditions is it exploiting that allows it to compete and establish on this site?

The unforeseen consequences of unthoughtful weed control may include replacement of herbicide-susceptible weeds with resistant strains, reduction in genetic resources, development of 'secondary pests' that had previously preferred the weed plant, reduction of food, shelter and breeding sites for beneficial organisms, and the erosion and loss of nutrients that may have been stored by weeds.

Reducing herbicide use

Any weed control action that is aimed at reducing herbicide input should start with a thorough consideration of these questions:
- What is a weed?
- What can this weed tell us about conditions on site?
- How many of this particular species can we tolerate?
- Can they be eliminated completely?
- Can the current species be manipulated or managed better than others that may exploit the opportunity if we control this species completely?
- What are the economic consequences of controlling or not controlling this weed? How will the weeds affect pests and diseases?

Only when these questions have been addressed should our attention be turned to the question of how to control them.

An ecological control program may use any of the following techniques:

- choice of crop and variety (for rapid establishment and competition)
- variation to the method of land preparation (cultivation, seed-bed finish, etc.)
- sowing and planting techniques (density of planting, planting configuration, etc.)
- fertility adjustments
- inter-row cultivation in the growing crop
- water management (e.g. restricting water availability by use of drippers)
- harvesting and seed saving (saving the best and most vigorous seed)
- sanitation and quarantine (preventing the movement and introduction of weeds)
- mulching with organic or inorganic materials
- use of grazing animals
- mowing, slashing
- use of intercropping, smother crops, living mulches, cover crops etc.
- hand-weeding, hoeing
- burning or thermal controls
- crop rotation
- biological controls including insects and pathogens
- organic herbicides such as vinegar or extracts of plant essential oils.

Fundamental questions for weed control:

What is a weed (generally or in this particular location)? What can this weed tell us about soil and environmental conditions on this site?

> How many of this particular species can we tolerate?
> Can this weed be eliminated completely?
> Can this weed be manipulated or managed better than any other weed that may exploit the opportunity if we control the first species completely?
> What are the economic consequences of controlling or not controlling this weed?
> How will this weed affect pests and diseases?

NOT SO GOOD-LOOKING

Unsightliness often turns up in a list of the characteristics of weeds. This is interesting because few weeds could be said to be unsightly per se — they are only green plants, after all. They may even be attractive flowering plants such as buttercups or dandelions and they may well grow where there would otherwise be unattractive bare soil.

Perhaps some weeds do affect the neatness and order of a landscape, but what if unsightliness is really about an inappropriate, outdated, un-ecological way of looking? This is not to defend weeds where they do harm, or to excuse anyone from cleaning up weeds that are bothering the neighbours. But what if an offended viticulturist discovers that the 'unsightly' oxalis growing *between* the vines makes a colourful cover crop *under* the vines; that it doesn't grow tall enough to poke into the canopy to interfere with the harvest; that it suppresses grasses and other weeds that would cause more harm; that it reduces the need for tractor time to mow or cultivate; and that dies down in summer and becomes mulch and does not compete with the vines for water?

Even with these advantages in evidence, some people will find it hard to overcome the perceptive barriers between their socialised view of weeds and a more ecological way of looking.

Seen from an environmental perspective, a few weeds under the fruit trees at the back of the yard are better than bare earth — and much better than soil with herbicide residues.

THE STORY OF HERBICIDES

Prior to the 1950s, chemical control of weeds was limited to a few simple products. Common salt, turpentine or diesel, inorganic arsenicals, boracic compounds, sulphate of iron or copper were sometimes used to kill weeds over relatively small acreages.

Major advances in herbicide science occurred between 1940 and 1945 in the United States as a by-product of chemical warfare research. This research led directly to the synthesis of the 'phenoxy', or hormone weed killers known as MCPA and 2,4-D. These were the first proven selective herbicides, capable of removing broadleaf weeds from lawns or cereal crops. Placed on the market in 1946, 2,4-D enjoyed spectacular sales.

During the '60s, herbicide sales increased at an average rate of 20 per cent per annum and by 1971 accounted for almost 50 per cent of world pesticide sales, especially due to development of novel herbicides suitable for use in almost all types of arable crops.

It is astounding that for so long after the arrival of herbicides there was great faith that they would eliminate weeds, that they were safe to use and that they would have few or no side effects. I went to many meetings of farmers and agriculture professionals where the gathering was divided on their views about safety of agricultural chemicals — those who advocated for safety precautions and those who protested, 'But they are safe'.

Strangely, these abandoners of caution pointed at my lot, the organic few, and at the occasional environmental and human safety campaigner, and tried to tell us we were 'unscientific'. We deserved this term because we did not accept the dictum of the chemical company, that glyphosate would become immediately safe when it touched the ground. They could not really explain how glyphosate might disappear, as if by magic, as the process of pesticide breakdown happens through multiple pathways over time. Depending upon the soil type, temperature and moisture range, and the quantity of pesticide used, these chemicals may be broken down by the action of sunlight, by gradual chemical decomposition (which may occur faster in warm, moist, acid soil), and by the action of particular soil organisms, chiefly bacteria. When the company said that glyphosate was inactivated upon touching the soil, they really meant that it was readily adsorbed onto the clay fraction of the soil and tightly bound. In fact, glyphosate may change soil chemistry by displacing cations (positively charged ions) that would otherwise remain attached to the clay particles, with the glyphosate molecule or its breakdown products detaching again from the soil as the chemistry changes.

Glyphosate residues are now sometimes found in food products, such as onions. Onions are sensitive to weed competition in their early growth, so herbicides are used. They are often grown in sandy soil, which means there is little clay to absorb the herbicide. Sometimes when conditions are right, that is in alkaline soils (onions don't mind that), and when it is overcast, dry and cool immediately after application, the herbicide can hang around long enough to get taken up. This is not to mention the effects on the user of the chemical at this stage.

Herbicides do not get rid of weeds

Herbicides are a useful 'band-aid' strategy for weed control — without them we would have a greater extent of weed infestation and the need for more drudge-worthy physical labour. Herbicides are a viable tool for some combinations of site and weed species and management options. Notwithstanding the importance of herbicides in some locations, herbicides do not eradicate weeds; they merely remove the problem temporarily.

Unfortunately, herbicides easily become the lazy option. We apply the chemical and get a dramatic visual response in a few days or a week, so it's easy to feel satisfied that we have done some useful, constructive work. Without follow-up activities, we are left with bare soil — which is the ultimate invitation for weeds to re-establish.

Because of the inevitability of evolutionary responses, we may even get worse weeds back — either hardier or harder-to-kill species, or herbicide-resistant versions of the same weed. Resistance develops because some plants have the ability to disable or breakdown the herbicide. When the herbicide removes their competition, plants with the ability to resist are favoured and soon become the dominant version of the weed.

Domestic gardeners are often unfamiliar with the important factors that must be considered when applying herbicides. Soil type, climatic conditions (temperature, rain, wind), weed type and stage of growth of the target plant are of utmost importance. The variety of chemical, the method of application and the calibration of equipment also make a significant difference to efficacy. Unfamiliarity with these factors can lead to frustration. Weeds get out of control, which in turn leads to increased dosage, which then speeds the time to resistance, which then requires more or stronger chemicals — and now we are on the treadmill. This treadmill is spinning off more negative side effects, such as non-target damage, contamination and human exposure.

Herbicides can do harm

It's easy to misuse herbicides through ignorance or as a result of unforseen environmental conditions. Ester herbicides cause volatile drift for hours after their use, and simazine and other persistent path-weeders can readily affect non-target plants, by chemical drift or via the soil.

All herbicides leave residues and breakdown products in the soil and many of these can harm plants, animals, insects and soil microbes. Pesticide manufacture also has a very high carbon footprint.

Herbicide use — a personal experience

When I was a young horticulturalist, I was asked to apply herbicides. Although I was studying horticulture, I had very little training in how to apply chemicals, and even less in how they worked and what the potential hazards might be. I decided I should learn how to use them safely and to protect myself from any potential negative impact. Unfortunately, I saw many colleagues who did not adopt this attitude and regularly put themselves at risk. Some covered their actions with brave banter about their invulnerability and, regrettably, some swallowed whole the constant message about safety that we often heard from chemical companies and government advisors.

Almost all of these safety claims have been proven wrong. Although I do not want to scaremonger and would prefer that people always used chemicals within accepted guidelines, the fact remains that chemical exposure is always bad and alternatives should always to be preferred.

When I was first starting out, I actually used the protective equipment when loading up the spray unit and I tried to follow the safety instructions carefully. Later I discovered that the 'use a little bit more to be sure' attitude was actually contributing to resistance and reducing the effectiveness of chemicals.

I became a lecturer in horticulture at TAFE and started to teach chemical safety and application courses. After leaving TAFE I worked as a contract presenter for a chemical-training program in my region, one of the few anywhere that targeted homeowners and small landholders with free safety advice. Altogether, I accumulated 20 years as a chemical safety trainer.

I also occasionally used chemicals in bush care and around the home property, but only in intractable situations. For example, I owned some steep rocky land in the Adelaide Hills that had serious woody weed infestations, including cotoneaster, holly, broom and gorse. All of these I could handle on flat land, but on the slope they could not be grazed or grubbed without serious risk of erosion. So I learned to use the cut-and-swab technique, which reduced the total amount of active ingredient used and was better for the environment. But there was another significant problem — even though it was the most targeted use possible, the risk of personal exposure was much greater. So it became necessary to develop safe handling systems.

I've trained many hundreds of volunteer bush carers over the years, who worked with local government, national parks, the National Trust, community groups and employment training programs. I was selected to deliver this training because of my professional involvement in catchment and roadside management, in broad-scale landscape revegetation and bushcare work, and for my conservation interests. All the while, I have continued to apply chemicals at home, albeit organically acceptable ones. Even natural pesticides are potentially harmful and should be treated with the same precautions as synthetic chemicals.

Throughout this time I have been amazed at the failure of many chemical users to adequately prepare for application. Look at it this way: most of us understand that if we hit our thumb with a hammer, it hurts. We call that acute pain. It is much harder to comprehend that chronic effects result from long-term exposure to chemicals. Continual exposure to small amounts can accumulate and exposure to multiple chemicals can also compound the negatives. It was easy for me as someone who observed the bush and knew about safety to find examples of poor practices and preparation. While the various authorities were saying, 'We know about the risks and train our workers', the evidence around me was contrary — the message had not sunk in.

When I trained chemical users who had previously obtained their S7 certificate or Pesticide Applicators Certificate, I suggested that the chemical dyes they were using were more toxic than some herbicides (and that food-grade vegetable dye was cheaper and just as effective), and when I suggested that perhaps they should not wash their protective gear in the same washing machine as the baby's nappies without a clean-down, or described how they might handle protective gear between shifts they often said, 'No one has ever told us that before.' The men always responded well because they were open to the concept of protecting women of child-bearing age and their kids. Yet somehow, they had almost never considered that they also contribute 50 per cent of the genetic material to the baby and that they should consider their own exposure from that perspective.

If I agreed with farmers and rural landowners that yes, sometimes herbicides are useful and appropriate, I could see a great relief descend upon them. I was giving them permission to use chemicals. Recognising that I was committed to a non-chemical world, they appreciated that this was a significant concession. Having conceded a role for chemicals, however, the problem was that when we looked closely at a particular treatment situation, we were likely to disagree about the urgency or applicability of chemical solutions.

Knowledge, of course, is also very important here. You need to not only know about the potential harmful impact of chemicals, but also how to tackle weeds using physical methods. Developing the ability to observe and critically assess is a vital skill for organic growers. For instance, non-indigenous (Eastern states) wattles are serious invaders of bushland near my home in the Mount Lofty Ranges, South Australia, but they are effectively removed by cutting them off at ground level, just above the crown root. Cut higher and the adventitious buds sprout prolifically, but these buds do not extend to the base of the stem. Cut close enough and there will be no regrowth.

The result of this experience is that I often start a development job on my property with the idea that I might use some synthetic herbicides if necessary. In reality — and after some satisfying labour — I am pleased at how easily weeds yield to knowledge and physical force. For many years now, I have only used synthetic herbicides for cut-and-swab applications to eradicate woody weeds when it is impossible to dig out the stump and roots.

An example of where I have used cut-and-swab (or drill-and-fill) technique in the garden was a cork elm (*Ulmus thomasii*). This invasive tree grew to about 15 metres in height, but was sprouting from roots 50 metres away, on the opposite side of the house. Clearly this was not a digging job. A little targeted herbicide and the tree died in one season, rather than taking years of cutting, digging and pulling.

Weed woes

There are many negative effects of weeds. Here are just a few. Weeds can:

- compete with garden or crop plants for light, space, water and soil nutrients
- attract pollinators away from crops
- release (allelopathic) chemicals into soil to inhibit the germination or growth of desirable plants
- parasitise garden and crop plants — for example, dodder (*Cuscuta* species)
- provide a host site for pests and pathogens
- reduce growth and yield of garden and crop plants
- crowd out more useful pasture species
- provide refuge for feral animals
- poison stock
- physically damage stock with sharp seeds or burrs
- damage and reduce the value of agricultural products — for example, with tainted milk, burred wool and contaminated seed crops
- clog waterways, water distribution channels, irrigation channels and drains
- pollute waterways with fallen leaves and organic matter
- reduce opportunities for recreational use of land or water
- reduce the functionality and increase cost of maintenance of turf and playing fields
- threaten infrastructure such as roads, powerlines and railways
- increase erosion by baring soil
- change the fire frequency and fuel load of bushland
- affect the germ plasm (genetic integrity) of crop plants and seed viability
- look unsightly.

GENETICALLY MODIFIED 'SUPERWEEDS'

Hybridisation (where two types of plant cross-pollinate to create another) can lead to harder-to-kill weeds. Cross-pollination between genetically modified (GM) crop plants and their wild and weedy relatives is inevitable and has the potential to create hybrid superweeds resistant to the most powerful weedkillers. Superweeds might incorporate genes that are resistant to weedkillers — and these genes may have come from GM crops engineered to be herbicide-tolerant.

As most native vegetation or plant-breeding buffs can tell you, hybridisation is more widespread and frequent than many people understand. Hybridisation will occur if adequate buffer zones, designed to stop pollen spreading from GM crops into the wild, are not strictly maintained.

HOW WEEDS GET AROUND

Weeds spread in many ways, including seed, spores, surface or underground runners, layering and rooting from broken stems and leaves.

All soils contain a vast reserve of weed seed in various stages of dormancy or germination. An individual dock plant can produce half a million seeds, and one large amaranth plant can produce 700,000 seeds. All annual weeds and some perennials spread by seed. Weeds that produce many seeds tend to have very small seeds, whereas weeds that make fewer seeds often have large seed. Seed may be very long-lived in the soil, lasting decades, and possibly even hundreds of years, in ideal conditions.

Some seeds, such as dandelion and thistle, are particularly adapted to wind distribution, possessing tiny 'parachute' attachments to help their travels. Sycamore seeds have large wings that catch the wind and cause them to flutter around, helicopter-style. Some weeds with wind-dispersed seeds, such as shepherd's purse, have capsules that open rapidly and project the small seed into the air to better capture a breeze.

Blackberry and mistletoe have seeds that still germinate after moving through the gut of a bird; mistletoe has a sticky surface so it can stay attached to a branch. Cleavers and burdock have tiny hooks that stick like Velcro to animal fur or clothing.

Birds spread weeds over long distances by transporting seed in mud attached to their body, and by passing them through their digestive system.

Spreading the seed

Weeds are spread by a wide variety of methods:
- **wind** blows the seed of thistles, dandelions, daisies, skeleton weed, as well as bracken fern spores
- **water** moves whole waterweeds, such as hyacinth, or seeds such as St John's wort, Bathurst burr and California thistle
- **birds** move fruit and seeds such as blackberry, boxthorn and blackberry nightshade
- **animal** hair and fur moves seeds such as dock, burrs, three-corner Jack, innocent weed, spear grass, barley grass and skeleton weed
- **animal dung** introduces weed seeds such as capeweed, thistles, salvation Jane, Cape tulip, dock and silver-leaf nightshade
- **vehicles** tyres or muddy animals move weeds such as dock, caltrop and skeleton weed
- **agricultural machinery** moves weeds such as dock, skeleton weed, sorrel, couch grass and convolvulus

> - **hay** moves seed such as capeweed, dock, thistle, barley grass and wild turnip
> - **pot plants** introduce weeds such as soursob and fumitory.

Roguing

Roguing is the practice of removing the seed heads of weeds before seeds mature. In some garden contexts it could be called deadheading. Use this technique to halt or reduce the further spread of weeds until you can find the time to deal with them in a more lasting way.

Roguing may be done by breaking off or pinching out flowers and seed heads by hand, with secateurs, or with mowers, slashers and brush-cutters (whipper-snippers).

WHICH WEEDS CAN YOU KEEP?

We need weeds to provide multiple environmental functions. These include soil protection and improvement, and habitat for birds, insects and other animals. The goal is to select the weeds that can provide these free services with a minimum of negative impact. Particularly, we want to end up with a suite of weeds that can be cleared away with minimum effort when required.

But it's not all good. Some weeds just have to go — such as those that take a great deal of effort to remove, or those that cause allergies or poisoning of stock and so on. Some weeds can sometimes (but not always) have negative impact, such as harbouring pests and disease. Dock can attract aphids, thistles and datura (*Datura stramonium*) can host lettuce necrotic yellows virus (LNYV), and shepherd's purse transmits root-knot nematodes. If LNYV is a problem in your district (if your lettuce plants turn to a slimy mess before they mature), don't let thistles grow near the lettuce patch.

What makes a weed ?

Here's a list of the accepted characteristics of a weed, compiled from various sources in the scientific literature on weeds:

1. They grow in an undesired location.
2. They have no special requirements for germination.
3. If they are a perennial, they have vigorous vegetative reproduction.
4. If they are a perennial, they have a brittle point at a lower node or at rhizomes or rootstocks.
5. If they are a perennial, they vigorously regenerate from severed rootstock.
6. Seeds germinate over a long period (seasonal and temporal).
7. They are self-pollinated, or if cross-pollinated do not need a specialised flower visitor.
8. They have only a short vegetative period before producing seeds.
9. They have special abilities that allow them to compete, such as rosette formation (a flat circular pattern of leaves in early stage of growth), or production of chemicals that inhibit other plants.
10. They grow wild and rank.
11. They are persistent and resistant to control and eradication.
12. They are often develop large populations.
13. They are useless, unwanted and undesirable.
14. They are harmful to humans, animals and crops.
15. They grow without being sown or cultivated.
16. They have a high reproductive capacity.

> 17. They are unsightly, causing disfigurement of the landscape.
> 18. They have a high tolerance for climate and soil variation.

KNOW YOUR TERMINOLOGY

It's important to know some simple botanical terms and concepts to help you agree on the target species and understand how it behaves.

Weed words and botanical names

All living things can be categorised and named according to an agreed scientific classification system. They are first assigned to broad categories (domain, kingdom, phylum, class) and then to progressively narrower groupings (family, genus, species) and given a unique name. The first name consists of the genus name and the second part is the species name. Some plants may also have a subspecies name, usually denoting a variety or cultivar of that species. This name appears last; in botanical reference books there may also be an indication of the person who originally classified and named the species. The convention for scientific names is that they should appear in italic type.

Genus (or the plural *genera*) refers to a group of closely related species. In botanical classification, genus comes above a species and below a family. For example, all roses belong to the genus *Rosa*. Genus names are capitalised.

Species is a fundamental category of the classification of living things. It comes below a genus and above a subspecies. It refers to a population made up of individuals that are capable of interbreeding (reproducing) and producing fertile young. A species group is also considered varied or different from other populations. The word 'species' is sometimes abbreviated to sp., or the plural spp., which is used to refer to all the species within a genus or all the representatives of that genus present. Species names are not capitalised. *Rosa alba* for example, is a species of rose.

WEED TYPES, GROWTH HABITS AND CONTROL
Ephemerals
Ephemerals are plants with short life cycles — between three weeks and several months. Ephemeral weeds often have the ability to go through more than one cycle of germination, flowering and seed production in a season or year, depending on favourable environmental conditions such as temperature and moisture. Ephemerals include weeds such as winter grass (*Poa annua*), shepherd's purse (*Capsella bursa-pastoris*) or spurge (*Euphorbia* species) and groundsel (*Senecio* species). There are many native and perennial senecio weeds, too.

Annuals
Annuals last one year only. They may be winter or summer plants when growing in northern Australia, but in southern regions there are few winter-growing annuals that become serious weeds.

Annual broadleaf weeds such as blackberry nightshade (*Solanum nigrum*) or Paterson's curse (*Echium* species) live for one season and produce one set of flowers. They have no underground storage organs. Some plants can change their growth patterns depending on their environment. Paterson's curse, for instance, can behave like a biennial (living two years) in South Australia, but will complete its lifecycle in one year in other areas. Because annuals usually live for only one season they rely upon seed production to reproduce. They must be controlled before they can set a new crop of seeds. Unchecked seed production can be very high. Fat hen (*Chenopodium album*) can produce 500,000 seeds per plant and amaranth (*Amaranthus* species) even more. When plants invest in high rates of seed production, the seed is generally only short-lived (three to five years), but the total quantity of seed is a major challenge. Longer-lived seeds are usually larger, have a hard coating and may contain high oil levels. Very long-lived seeds can remain viable for many decades. Cultivation of soil continually brings new seeds to the soil surface. Small seeds need to be within the top several centimetres of soil to germinate, but larger seeds can germinate from a greater depth.

Typical broadleaf shape

Winter annuals
Winter grass (*Poa annua*)
Fumitory (*Fumaria* species)
Chickweed (*Stellaria media*)
Petty spurge (*Euphorbia peplus*)

Summer annuals
Barnyard grass (*Echinochloa crus-galli*)
Caltrop (*Tribulus terrestris*)
Purslane (*Portulaca oleracea*)

Grassy annuals develop fibrous root systems that are capable of getting a good hold on the ground. Perennial grasses are hard to pull out by hand or to control mechanically (for instance with a rotary hoe or tractor-drawn cultivator). Annual grasses do not have time to establish an extensive root system and are easier to pull by hand. The growing point of grasses is located at or below the soil surface, so mowing doesn't generally kill them, although their growth and rate of seed production may be retarded.

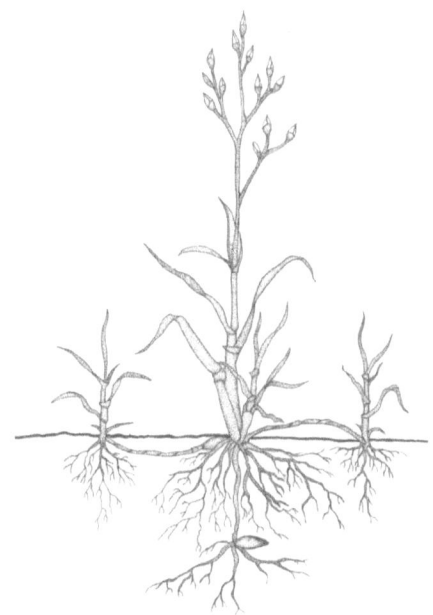

A typical grass plant

There are annual and perennial grasses. Wild oats (*Avena fatua*) and bearded oats (*Avena barbata*) are annual grasses.

Because the growing tips of grasses are well protected, they grow back quickly after mowing; areas that are regularly mown often become dominated by grass.

Biennials

Biennials take two years to complete their life cycle. In the first year the seeds germinate, usually in spring, and form a rosette or crown of leaves and a fleshy taproot. In the second year they send up a flower stalk, usually in the spring. Biennials die after seed production.

Annuals and biennials grow from seed, but biennials survive over one winter as a taproot, with little or no top growth.

Dandelion is an example of a rosette

Perennials

Perennials may live for many years and do not necessarily die after flowering. They may grow from seed or underground parts or both. Their roots may be very persistent, possibly modified into rhizomes or tubers, and the above-ground parts may die away each year in summer or winter. Some perennial weeds, such as couch and kikuyu, contain significant starch reserves in their underground parts that can repeatedly give rise to strongly growing new growth.

Perennials may produce seeds each year, and the plant that produces the seeds can remain intact for many years. Other perennials may grow for many years, then flower once and die.

Herbaceous perennials die back to their roots sometime after producing new seeds, but re-appear the next season. They survive over winter in underground parts such as taproots, rhizomes, tubers, bulbs or corms. Herbaceous perennials such as dock may produce an annual flower spike that dies back each year. Another herbaceous perennial is bracken fern, which can survive over winter with food stored in rhizomes. It's important to remember that bracken these days is considered a native, so is not a weed if growing in native vegetation.

Grass-like perennials

Grasses are monocotyledons, that is, they produce only one leaf per seed when they germinate. They also have long narrow leaves with parallel veins. Most non-grasses (dicotyledons) have two leaves per seed and broader leaves with a network of veins. There are some non-grass monocots, but they tend to look quite grass-like. These plants may grow from bulbs and corms, for example, watsonia, or they may be sedges from the Cyperaceae family and identified by a stem that is triangular in cross-section, for example nutgrass (*Cyperus rotundus*). Other non-grass monocots include lilies, irises, orchids and palms.

Note: Pines vary (from species to species) from one to multiple cotyledons, so they are classified separately as multi-cotyledons.

Woody perennials

Woody perennials produce permanent, above ground woody stems and may take form as vines, shrubs or trees. They may propagate from seed and may also have dormant buds at the crown root or in roots near the soil surface from which they can regrow if the tops are removed by felling or fire. This practice is known as *coppicing*, if growth comes from the stem, or *suckering* if growth arises from roots.

Control of perennials

Some perennials are harder to control than annuals because they have the time to develop extensive root systems and are more likely to regenerate from underground parts than annuals. Digging over or chopping perennials with a hoe only spreads the roots or rhizomes from which the weed will regrow. Perennials therefore require special attention.

Pulling is rarely effective, because perennials have brittle points at a low node or underground; they easily break in pieces and each piece is capable of growing. Frequent repeated pulling may reduce or control perennials in small areas if you get all the root material out.

Perennials generally require digging. If possible, use forks, trowels, bulb diggers and other tools that do not require completely turning soil over. If soil must be turned, add compost and then cover with mulch or plant the area with groundcovers or garden plants as soon as possible.

Where perennial weeds are thoroughly intermixed with herbaceous or woody plants, digging may be impossible without completely renovating the bed. This means digging over the entire patch, lifting any plants small enough to be lifted and carefully pulling out every trace of root or rhizome from the root ball of the garden plants.

If pulling is to be effective control method it must stop the cycle of seed production, so regularly revisit the area to remove weed regrowth.

Succulents

Succulents are plants that retain water in their tissues (leaves, stems or roots) in order to survive arid climates or saline soils. They often have a fleshy appearance. Most succulents have water-saving features such as reduced or cylindrical leaves, few stomata (tiny pores on the underside of leaves where gases are exchanged), absence of leaves (the stem becomes the photosynthetic part), a compact or columnar shape, and waxy or hairy surfaces to increase humidity around the plant. The best known examples of succulents are cacti. Succulents can be annuals or perennials.

Variability of life cycle

Some biennials and ephemerals can vary in their life cycle locally. For instance, if biennials germinate early and go through a cold snap they may become vernalised (hastened towards development and flowering by exposure to low temperatures) and behave like annuals; if they are mowed repeatedly and prevented from flowering, they may behave like perennials.

SEXUAL REPRODUCTION

Seed is the result of sexual reproduction in angiosperms (flowering plants). Flowers contain the male and female sexual organs, including the ovary. During sexual reproduction, characteristics can be inherited from the male and female gametes, resulting in greater genetic diversity.

Weeds may employ a wide range of seed production and dispersal strategies to ensure they are effectively distributed throughout their environment. These include:

- production of many seeds
- long seed life and seed dormancy
- irregular germination of seed (not all at once) and germination over a long seasonal period
- attractiveness of fruit or seed to birds and other animals
- sticky or barbed appendages to catch in fur and feathers
- parachute attachments to catch the wind.

Let's talk about sex

Flowers are the reproductive organs of plants that reproduce sexually. In many flowering plants, both female and male reproductive organs are contained within the one flower. The female organ — the pistil — is made up of a stigma, style and ovary. The male fertilising organ is the stamen, typically consisting of an anther and a filament. The anther produces pollen (the male sex cells). The pistil and stamen are usually surrounded by one or more petals (often the colourful part) known as the corolla, and this is surrounded by a whorl of sepals (usually green) called the calyx. Individual flowers are supported on a pedicel and inflorescences (more than one flower appearing together) are supported by a peduncle. In some plant populations, the male and female reproductive structures are in separate individuals (dioecious).

Seeds are the product of sexual reproduction. They produce a plant with different characteristics to the parent plants due to genetic variability arising from sexual reproduction.

Seed dormancy refers to the ability of seeds to delay germination. Many different processes, including access to light, oxygen, exposure to high or low temperature and chemical ripening, can break seed dormancy. The germination trigger may not occur at the same time for all seeds because it is dependent on how they are distributed throughout the soil during the dormancy period. Some seeds may germinate in each season, but others survive much longer. This ensures that one bad season cannot terminate the population. Seed longevity refers to the ability of seed to survive in the soil, sometimes for very long periods. For example, nutgrass (*Cyperus rotundus*) or Canada thistle (*Cirsium arvense*) seed may survive for more than 20 years.

VEGETATIVE REPRODUCTION

Vegetative reproduction arises from taproots, rhizomes, tubers, bulbs and corms or other organs. Plants that reproduce from vegetative growth are effectively clones with little genetic diversity, although inevitably there is some variation across a large population or between populations.

Roots, runners and rhizomes

Perennial weeds often travel and spread by vegetative growth. They may also produce seed, but this is just an additional strategy and vigorously growing parts tend to be the more important method of distribution. Couch grass and kikuyu are the most common examples of weeds that spread rapidly from runners and stolons. The rhizomes of the common horsetail (*Equisetum arvense*) are notorious for their ability to grow underground for long distances, sometimes even passing beneath bitumen roads before they emerge again. These rhizomes are exceptionally hard to kill, even with herbicides.

Canada thistle (*Cirsium arvense*) can send out lateral roots at a depth of 1 metre in the soil and is capable of growing from a piece of root only 2.5 centimetres long. A thistle planted from a cutting was measured two years later and had grown a 20-metre root system.

Terminology of vegetative reproductive parts

Corms are short, vertical, swollen underground stems that give rise directly to leaves and flowers in the spring or autumn. They have a dormant period — usually winter but sometimes summer — and can produce adventitious roots. The outer layer is covered with papery leaves (tunic leaves) that protect the corm from water loss or insect attack. Corms can be distinguished from bulbs by the lack of fleshy scales. Watsonia and crocus grow from corms.

Bulbs are thickened, fleshy underground terminal buds that are starch-storage organs. Bulbils (smaller bulblike structures) may also form in the flowers or in the leaf axis. Bulbs have layers of 'scales' that are actually modified leaves. Onions are bulbs.

Stolons are modified horizontal stems that grow at or just below the soil surface and give rise to new plants from adventitious roots at the ends of the stolon or at nodes. Stolons are often called runners. Wandering Jew (*Tradescantia* species) is an example of a plant that grows from stolons.

Adventitious roots are roots that arise from unexpected parts of the plant — for example, from stems, leaves or old woody roots.

Rhizomes are horizontal underground stems capable of giving rise to new plants. Rhizomes are the main stem of the plant, whereas stolons arise from the main stem. Occasionally rhizomes for example iris or ginger, may be found at or just above the soil surface.

Tubers are underground starch storage-organs that arise by the thickening of a stolon or rhizome. A potato is a tuber arising from a modified stolon.

Layering occurs when a stem produces aerial roots or conventional roots when it touches the ground. Blackberry is an excellent example of a plant that layers freely, and blackberry thickets can develop rapidly due to long stems falling over and layering where they are in contact with the ground.

What is a weed?

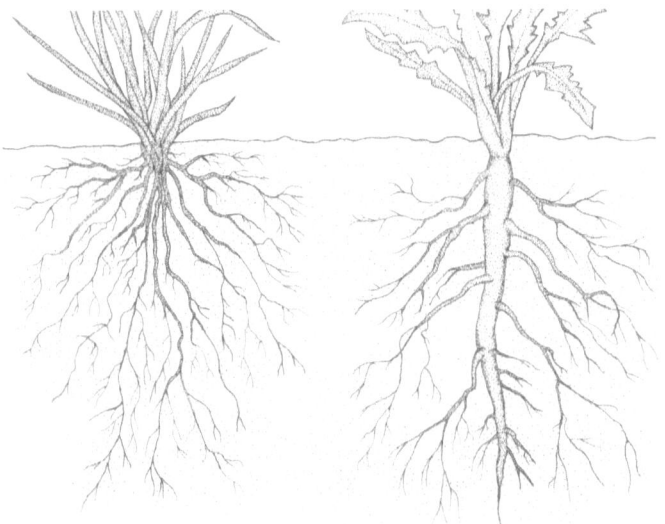

A fibrous root system (left) and a taproot system

2
Take control

From one perspective, weeds are just very successful plants. They are good at getting around, they're great at competing for space and they produce lots of seed or vegetative propagules. This section deals with methods that try to beat weeds at their own game. The most 'biological' and therefore the most truly organic strategy is to use plants to occupy garden space and keep weeds at bay. We may even select certain 'weeds' or other plants to work for us by turning them into green manures, cover crops, smother crops or groundcovers.

> ## Tim's top 10 tips for organic weed control
>
> 1. Always use quarantine and hygiene practices to keep the garden free of new weeds.
> 2. Prevent existing weeds from seeding or spreading.
> 3. Work strategically and to a plan. Concentrate efforts on a smaller area and achieve the best possible control before moving to the next area.
> 4. Work from an edge. Start with the area of least infestation and move towards the area of greater density.

5. Fill spaces created by weed control with seeds, plants or mulch.
6. Regular and consistent beats spasmodic every time. Even if you can only manage 10 minutes per day, you will gradually reclaim more land if you work efficiently from an edge.
7. Hand weeding is the most accurate way to control weeds because it is effective at completely removing weeds. It therefore is the most time-efficient method in the long run.
8. Work out which weeds you can work with and which ones must be eradicated. Work on weeds that you don't want as the main priority.
9. **Now** is the best time to carry out weed control. If you see a weed you don't want, pull or dig it out or pull off the seed heads.
10. Be responsible for your weeds. Don't cause problems for neighbours or allow weeds to spread to bushland.

PLANT-BASED WEED CONTROL STRATEGIES

Preventative methods are often undervalued, but are actually critically important in stopping weeds from invading or spreading. They are sometimes called 'management controls'.

Quarantine and hygiene

Keep seed out of your garden or paddock. Clean vehicles, tools and socks after returning from weedy areas. Select clean sources of mulch, compost, garden soil and potted plants. Always consider the risk from importing mulching materials. Put suspect organic material through an aerobic compost process prior to applying to the soil. Many different methods of composting are covered in

Composting: The Ultimate Organic Guide to Recycling Your Garden (2008, ABC Books, Sydney).

Materials such as bark and wood chips are generally clean; lucerne is good also, whereas cereal and pea straw from bales will often give rise to grasses and germinating peas. Cereals and peas growing in the mulch are easily pulled while they are small and in some situations can become a useful cover crop or green manure. Meadow hay, however, is a high-risk material because it may have a broader species content. Burrs and thistles are sometimes imported in mulching hay so ask about the weed history of the paddock it came from. Sometimes cheap mulch straw is available from rain spoiled or imperfectly baled material but it is worth investigating the source. Take one bale home, spread it out, water it and see what germinates. If it is relatively weed free after three weeks, with no serious weed species present, it should be safe to import a greater quantity. New weeds may come with the change of season, so be alert.

Bagged straw and other bagged mulch products should not contain weed seeds. The most reliably weed-free organic mulches are seaweed, shredded paper, leaves (such as autumn leaves or native leaves collected from weed-free areas) or processed materials such as sawdust, coir, fruit, olive or other pulps and meals.

Keep a close watch

It's always worthwhile taking a precautionary walk around the garden, keeping an eye out for new or rare weeds. Carry a pair of weed-pulling gloves and a trowel or other appropriate tool on your forays. The focus here is on the weeds you have not seen or the ones you really don't want and have nearly exterminated. Stop them before they produce seeds or rhizomes.

Take weeds with seeds attached to the compost immediately before they can spread. Be sure to compost perennial weeds carefully, placing the weedy material in the centre of a hot heap, or dehydrate weeds on a garden path before adding them to the compost. Weeds with a very high seed load can be placed in a plastic bag to rot before composting. Very serious weeds should be bagged and placed in the hard rubbish.

The most important weed control strategy is often simply to stop seed production by whatever means possible.

Prevention is better than cure
- Choose garden plants that are unlikely to become weeds in your area
- Inspect potted plants at the nursery and reject pots with weeds
- Purchase quality seed from reputable retailers. Beware of plants purchased from roadside stalls, markets and garage sales. Inspect them closely, ask appropriate questions and keep an eye on them when you get them home
- Only purchase top-quality garden soil from reliable suppliers
- Remove potentially weedy plants
- Dispose of garden waste carefully in the compost, green waste or council dump
- Do not mow when weeds are seeding — mow before they produce mature seed
- Compost animal manures before using, especially horse manure
- Plant species and varieties that are suited to your location and that can compete with weeds
- Use mulch or green manures and avoid bare soil
- If feeding suspect grain or hay to stock, keep them in a quarantine paddock until they void the seed. This prevents distribution across the whole property
- Stop weeds from producing seed by taking action before seeds are mature. Remove mature seed heads entirely from the area.

PLANNING FOR CROP PLANTS

Thorough planning before planting out a crop can have a significant impact upon the type and number of weeds that might eventuate in an area and how vigorously they grow.

Choice of crop variety Choose competitive varieties of crop or ornamental plants, especially favouring those with rapid early establishment.

Prepare the seedbed Consider no-till planting methods such as mulch gardens. If tilling the soil, leave time for follow-up cultivation (*see* stale seedbed page 99).

Plan the rotation Alternate strongly competitive crops with those that have faster establishment, more leaf and root production and allelopathic residues.

Sow in rows or blocks The access around plants for tools will be much easier.

Plant rather than sow Sowing means vegetable crops will be in the vulnerable bare-soil situation with a low leaf-to-area index for longer. Grow seedlings in flats and pots, and then transplant them to reduce the time required for weeding.

Plant closely Plants that form a canopy can be intentionally grown close together; for example, you can plant three rows of broccoli or cauliflower to a bed rather than two. The middle row is offset to the outside rows to form a check-row planting pattern. Cauliflower heads may be smaller, but the same or greater weight should be possible from the same area.

Prevent weed seed production Remove seed heads before seeds develop or mature. Use mowers, slashers, hand tools or grazing animals.

Use the same planning principles for perennial plants: choose healthy plants and suitable varieties, take care when planting, plant close to establish a canopy and stop weeds from producing seed. Mulch is often a suitable precaution for perennial plantings.

PLANT CLOSE AND USE THE THINNINGS

Use the recommended planting distance between the rows, but plant densely within the row. This leaves room to work with a hoe between the rows while the close planting distance inside the row crowds the weeds out. The thinnings from the rows are often quite edible. Try this method with spinach, onion, beetroot, any of the brassicas (use the leaves) and any salad greens.

CROP ROTATION

Crop rotation offers many benefits for organic growers; suppression of weeds is only one reason to practise it. Weakly competitive plants may be rotated with strongly competitive ones. Competitiveness is usually based upon a combination of characteristics such as early establishment, dense leaf coverage, strongly growing root systems, climbing or rambling habit and sometimes allelopathic effects.

Some examples of weakly competitive plants include carrots, young lettuce and onions, while spinach and most brassicas are strongly competitive.

A thickly sown green manure can provide strong competition to many weeds. Use single or mixed sowings of barley (*Hordeum vulgare*), oats (*Avena sativa*), faba (fava or broad) beans (*Vicia faba*), vetch (*Vicia villosa*), clovers (*Trifolium* species), mustard (*Brassica* species) or any other plant that grows well in your garden and can be controlled before it takes over.

If naturalised weeds serve this function, they will do just fine. The only condition must be that you can control them by mowing and mulching, chopping them into the soil or carting them off to the compost heap before they set seed.

There are many different versions of rotations for the vegetable garden but a standard rotation is:

Year 1 Legumes: peas (*Pisum sativum*), beans (*Phaseolus* or *Vigna* species), vetch (*Vicia* species)

Year 2 Heavy feeding crops: corn (*Zea mays*) or brassicas such as cabbage, broccoli, kale (*Brassica* species)

Year 3 Root vegetables: carrots (*Daucus* species), parsnip (*Pastinaca sativa*), beetroot (*Beta vulgaris*)

Year 4 Potatoes (*Solanum tuberosum*)

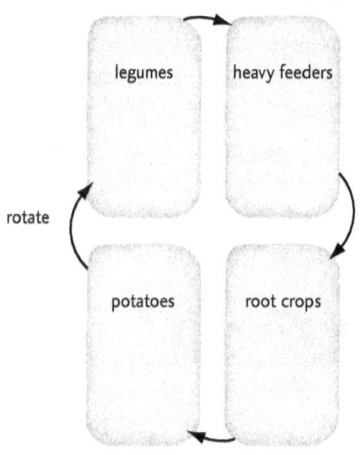

Common four-part vegetable rotation

PLANTING METHODS
Raised beds

Raised beds are easier to weed and therefore it's easier to prevent new weeds from invading them. They are a useful strategy where the garden adjoins a lawn. It is also possible to start raised beds over the top of weed infestations. To do this you will need to take several precautions. Pull, grub or mow the area to remove as much weed material as possible and then lay a porous weed mat barrier fabric under the beds. Finally, control the weeds on pathways with mulch or gravel to stop reinvasion.

Several layers of thick cardboard may also work under the beds, especially if the beds are high enough and the weeds underneath are not too aggressive. The cardboard will break down over time, so make sure enough layers of cardboard are used to provide a barrier until weeds have exhausted themselves trying to grow through.

The raised beds should be at least 15 centimetres off the ground to stop weeds, but persistent weeds such as oxalis will grow through much more soil and can only be stopped with an adequate barrier laid under the bed.

Beds should be narrow enough to allow easy access to the centre of the bed from either side (about 1.5 to 2 metres). Take care to avoid bringing in new weed seed if you are importing soil into the beds. Mix soil with compost and allow four to six weeks (or longer) for the beds to settle and weeds to germinate before planting the crop.

Raised beds made in this way and supplied with adequate compost should never need digging. Because they are not walked on or driven over, the soil should remain loose and friable so that weeds are easily pulled. Do not turn soil in the beds over; just add compost to the surface. This will prevent seeds being exposed to light and therefore primed to germinate.

Use seedlings, not seed
Grow seedlings in pots rather than in soil. This leaves the soil exposed for a shorter period while transplanted seedlings establish a complete canopy over the ground. Some crops such as carrots need to be grown from seed. Use the stale seedbed technique described below for sowing seed.

Undersowing
Undersowing crops with a 'living mulch' of low growing plants protects the soil from sun and intense rain, increases and recycles organic matter, produces good soil structure and suppresses germinating weeds. It may also have other valuable outcomes for desirable crop and garden plants, such as encouraging beneficial insects.

Low-growing and spreading plants are ideal for undersowing, such as prostrate clover and medics (*Medicago* species), purslane (*Portulaca oleracea*), chickweed (*Stellaria media*) and cress (*Lepidium sativum*). Plants with taproots are ideal, because deep roots offer less competition to the main crop plant, as well as recycling nutrients and moisture back through the soil profile. When you need to remove tap-rooted plants with a rosette shape, a few pulls or chops with the hoe clears a broad area of soil. Grasses require many tugs or chops to clear the same space, and shallow fibrous grass roots compete in the same soil zone as garden plants.

Cover-cropping
Cover-cropping is really the ultimate organic weed control technique because it is the most 'biological' method possible. It outwits weeds before they establish, using techniques that we usually associate with weeds. The method of hand-pulling that I use most often, described on page 89, uses self-seeded plants to create the plant cover, and provides a ready source of green material for compost whenever you need to thin out the cover crop. Living

mulches require adequate soil fertility so they do not compete with the garden or crop plants.

COVER CROPS
Clever Clover
CSIRO scientist Richard Stirzaker developed a special cover-cropping system, called clever clover, although some Tasmanian small-scale certified organic vegetable producers have used a similar system for many years. Thanks to Stirzaker, it is possible to purchase clever clover seed mixes in garden and commercial-size packets.

I use a version of clever clover where the garden area is first sown down to a suitable variety of clover. Strips of the clover are then removed and the crop rows planted. The creeping clovers then grow back to cover the bare soil and form a living mulch.

To understand the theory well, we can use the concept of leaf-to-area index. Young crop plants have a low area of leaf compared to the area of bare soil. This bare soil is easily colonised by weeds that can exploit the available sunlight, moisture and nutrients. As the crop grows, the area of leaf increases. With very leafy plants, such as the brassicas and spinach or zucchini, they eventually reach a leaf area at which they provide sufficient shade and smothering to suppress small germinating weeds. The cabbage family is an excellent example of this; they need some hoeing while young, but easily produce enough size and coverage to be quite self-sufficient later in life. In the third trimester of their growth, weed control activities will rarely be economically rewarded, except perhaps for roguing the seed heads of larger weeds emerging from the canopy of brassica plants.

Returning to the clever clover system, the area cleared prior to planting the main crop has to be wide enough so that by the time the clover has grown back over, the crop plant will be of a sufficient height and leaf-to-area index that it can successfully compete with the clover. The system then delivers primarily beneficial outcomes, such as free nitrogen, soil cover and protection, organic matter and nutrient cycling, as well as attracting beneficial insects.

Polyculture

Mixed cropping, or polyculture, uses a similar approach to the clever clover system, but productive plants fill more of the space and appropriate combinations of plants create their own suppressive soil cover to limit germination and establishment of weeds. Traditional plant mixes include sweet corn (*Zea mays*), beans (*Phaseolus* species and *Vigna* species) and squash (*Curcubita* species); leeks (*Allium ampeloprasum*) and celery (*Apium graveolens*); and tomato (*Lycopersicon esculentum*) and basil (*Ocimum basilicum*). In the tropics, try taro (*Alocasia macrorrhiza*), yam (*Dioscorea* species) and sweet potatoes (*Ipomoea batatas*).

Shade tolerance

In order for cover crops to remain in place under the main growing crop, some shade tolerance is necessary. Many white clovers, red clover, native medics and prostrate saltbush (*Atriplex* species) handle shady conditions well.

In tropical areas legumes such as pinto peanut (*Arachis pintoi*) handle dense shade and still produce a thick prostrate groundcover. Many other rambling legumes are also suitable, including velvet bean (*Mucuna pruriens*), but they may need to be cut back or unwound if they begin to climb garden plants. Pinto stays very flat.

Avoid water competition

In southern Australia, winter-growing cover crops such as cereal grasses and broad beans will not compete for water with the main crop. Some useful cover crops such as strawberry clover and native medics will die back in spring and summer as a result of high temperatures or natural senescence. Plants that regrow during spring and summer, such as white clover and subterranean clover, must be kept closely mown to restrict their competition for water.

Allelopathic plants

Some plant mixes suppress weeds primarily by competition and smothering, but some produce root exudates or leak chemicals from their decomposing residues that chemically inhibit the germination, growth or maturity of other plants (or similarly affect insects). The technical word for this interaction is allelopathy. Relevant examples of allelopathy include the use of species such as cereal rye (*Secale cereale*) and oats (*Avena* species), which can be both smothering (winter rye grows tall and produces a significant quantity of tough biomass) and can also chemically suppress germination of weeds. Rye will also chemically inhibit the growth of many small seedling-stage weeds such as fat hen (*Chenopodium album*).

Decomposing residues from these crops may also inhibit the early growth of susceptible vegetable and flower crops such as lettuce (*Lactuca sativa*), so it is necessary to wait three weeks after cutting or incorporating them before planting. If soil moisture is not adequate for quick breakdown of residues by microbes, a longer period may be required. Using advanced seedlings may also help the new crop get established. In the case of cover crops such as oats, the inhibiting chemicals are produced in the roots, therefore a lay period is required even if the crop residues are left on the soil surface and are not incorporated.

In northern Australia, sorghum and sudax grasses (*Sorghum* species) are very suppressive cover crops that also work chemically via a root exudate called sorgoleone (SGL). SGL is one of the strongest allelopathic chemicals and has an effect comparable with some synthetic herbicides. Leafy material from these crops will suppress nematodes if incorporated into the soil. Residues of other plants, for example mustard, contain glucosinolates that break down in the soil to isothiocyanates that prevent germination or kill young seedlings.

The allelopathic effect can be imported into the garden. Plants that naturally suppress weeds underneath, such as wormwood (*Artemisia absinthium*) and rosemary (*Rosmarinus officinalis*), can be grown in hedgerows and the pruned material chopped up and used to mulch problem weeds.

Tim's eight great benefits of cover crops

1. They produce large leaf area or rambling growth that can be used as smother crops to control weeds.
2. They may produce plant residues that provide mulch for the soil.
3. They attract beneficial insects into the garden to biologically control pests.
4. Some varieties include plants with allelopathic effects that inhibit weed growth or pest development (for example, mustard used as a soil fumigant or marigold to control nematodes).
5. They add organic matter directly to the soil from green manure roots, thereby encouraging microbial activity and creating a good soil structure.
6. They capture (sequester) and eventually recycle nutrients that might otherwise leach over winter.
7. They decrease infiltration time for water, thereby capturing more water into the soil profile.
8. They hold soil in place and reduce (or even eliminate) erosion, and protect water quality.

Cover crops and insect pests

Cover crops interact with every aspect of the farm and garden. The study of ecological interactions in cultivated fields, known as agroecology, reveals that it's possible to manipulate these interactions to create positive outcomes. Just some of the ways we can use cover crops to good effect include:

- restoring soil biology that has been destroyed by repeated cultivation, removal of plant cover, burning or crop residues and synthetic fertilisers and pesticides
- encouraging beneficial insects and other predators or parasitoids (an insect whose larvae live inside or attached to a single host, eventually consuming and killing it).

Landscapes with lots of diversity are much more hospitable for predators and parasitoids because they provide sites for hunting, resting, breeding and feeding. To fully comprehend this system it is necessary to know that many parasitoid insects, such as common hunting wasps, lay eggs in pests that eventually hatch to produce larvae that actually kill the host. The adults of these parasitoids consume pollen and nectar. Some hunting insects consume honeydew in certain life stages. Only diverse landscapes can produce the total resources necessary to maintain a sufficiently high population of beneficial insects to provide year-round control of pests.

It is therefore useful to diversify gardens in many different ways, including incorporating sequentially flowering trees and shrubs, as well as occupying what would otherwise be waste spaces with green manure and cover crops throughout the year. In this system, cover crops become much more than a winter strategy only and there may even be good reason to leave patches of green manures and cover crops (including naturalised or volunteer vegetation) unmown as habitat. Many commercial organic farmers rely on the slashing of cover crops and green manure to provide organic matter in situ, but they would never consider mowing the entire property in one tranche; they mow every second row, or leave strips untouched to provide continuous habitat.

In this system, weeds (that is, naturalised or volunteer plants) can be seen to be highly desirable by providing multiple functions that promote total garden health. It's necessary, of course, to evaluate the species composition of the naturalised vegetation to make sure that it doesn't include potentially rampant plants that might take over. Try to provide a species composition that is productive and manageable.

> Use mixtures of plant species to create diversified cover crops and green manures. This will help you gain the maximum effects from suppressive top growth, root exudates, predatory insects and mulch or incorporated green manure when the cover crop is mown or chopped in. Experiment with plant combinations that work for you, but species that are commonly found in mixes include hairy vetch, strawberry, white and sweet clover, ryegrass, broad beans and field peas.

Studies of agroecology not only reveal positive interaction between cover crops and beneficial insects, they also reveal that some weedy species are much more likely to host pest insects. The larvae of the vegetable weevil (*Listrodere* species) feed on marshmallow and capeweed, and many plant-sucking bugs feed on fleabane, capeweed and thistles.

Cover crops to try

White flowering sweet alyssum (*Lobularia maritima*) makes an excellent fast-spreading cover crop in the vegetable garden or vineyard. It is low-growing, grows easily from seed, is attractive to the eye, encourages beneficial insects, is perennial and self-seeds but is easy to pull if it encroaches too far or if you want to rejuvenate the bed. Coloured alyssum is less vigorous and not nearly as popular with wasps and hoverflies. Alyssum grows in most soil types in full sun or partial shade.

Baby's tears (*Soleirolia soleirolii*) grows to only 5 centimetres. It is excellent for using in rockeries, in cracks in crazy paving and as a cover crop for plants in pots. It forms an attractive low carpet effect. Aboveground growth is killed by frost but quickly recovers in spring.

Borage (*Borago officinalis*) is a little taller than most cover crops but is good under fruit trees in unused areas. The flowers look great in a salad or dessert.

Corsican mint (*Mentha requienii*) is possibly the lowest growing, ground-covering plant, rising to about 1 centimetre. It sits flat against the soil, provides excellent coverage and makes an attractive low carpet effect. It is well suited to growing in cracks in crazy paving and as a cover crop underneath other plants in pots (although it grows much better if it gets some sun for part of the day). It produces a wonderful minty fragrance when touched.

Dandelion (*Taraxacum officinale*) and **cat's ear** (*Hypochaeris radicata*) are both low-growing plants that can tolerate mowing. Both are considered weeds but when kept small and low they make a satisfactory cover crop. Managing these types of plants is about manipulating plant density and the size of the total population. If you can keep them within controllable limits you may not have eradicated the plant, but you may have solved the problem. Dandelion is attractive to the eye and to beneficial insects. It has a taproot that opens up compacted soil and is generally a soil-improver. Another bonus is that dandelion is edible. The leaves are great in salad.

Dandelion is also adaptable to a mowing regime and can

> Simply put, if you can get some use out of a plant and manage it so it doesn't take over, you can safely reclassify it. It's no longer a weed if you put it to use.

set seed under mower height, but the total number of mature seeds will be greatly reduced.

Gotukola (*Centella asiatica*) is native to northern Australian as well as Asia. It is an edible and medicinal plant that grows from creeping stolons in wet areas. Use the young leaves like any leafy green salad plant. Gotukola is ideal as a cover crop under vegetables, flowers and garden plants in tropical regions.

Nettles (*Urtica urens*) — yes, stinging nettles (the annual ones) — make an excellent cover crop. Mow or slash to keep them low. Nettles are great soil improvers. They are much less stingy when they are young or are regrowing from cutting.

New Zealand spinach (*Tetragonia tetragonoides*), otherwise known as Warrigal greens, is a short-lived perennial. It is an edible native of New Zealand and Australia. The leaves do contain toxic oxalates, so it's best to blanch them first before using them in cooking.

Pennyroyal (*Mentha pulegium*) is very low growing (3 centimetres) and hardy. It gives off a strong fragrance when walked on. Pennyroyal prefers moist locations.

Rocket or **arugula** (*Eruca versicaria*) is another edible crop plant that works well as a cover crop, especially as a short-term space filler in bare areas that have been opened up in the garden.

Stinking roger (*Tagetes minuta*) can be a weed in some gardens because it does seed profusely and some people do not like its smell (hence the name). It is reasonably easy to pull, repels pest insects and nematodes, and makes a good canopy to smother weeds.

Mixed herbs, especially prostrate forms of edible herbs such as marjoram and thyme, make excellent cover crops that repel pests from brassica and other long-lived crops. Basil goes very well with tomatoes.

There is no reason why any of these species have to be used alone. Mix them together in any combination that works for you.

Give it a go! Want to try a favourite plant as a cover crop? Give it a go. Start on a small area and be prepared to chase down plants that become too rampant. You could find that any attractive garden plant or weed can be converted to use as a cover crop.

Spot the difference between green manure and cover crop?

Green manures are grown for soil improvement and specifically for addition of organic matter to the soil (although they may produce other benefits). They are either slashed to the soil surface or tilled into the ground.

Cover crops are usually grown for multiple purposes, including protecting soil from erosion, adding organic matter, encouraging biological activity in soil, recycling nutrients and providing habitat for beneficial insects. They do not need to be slashed or incorporated and may sometimes complete their life cycle naturally or be allowed to reseed. They may be long-lived; cover crops may be a permanent feature under perennial vegetation such as vines or orchard trees.

GREEN MANURE

Green manure refers to a crop grown specifically for ploughing or turning back into the soil. They are mainly used for the purpose of soil protection or weed control but can also function as cover crops.

Green manures are usually turned in when still green and fresh, or while they are still actively growing. They may also be slashed or mulched and left on the soil surface rather than being incorporated.

Green manures are useful to organic gardeners because they:
- provide organic matter and humus to the soil
- prevent excess nitrates and other mobile nutrients from leaching through the soil
- maintain soil cover and prevent erosion
- improve the physical condition of the soil
- assist in the control of weeds and plant diseases
- can dry boggy soil, especially in warm and humid climates.

Choose your species

Many species are suitable for use as a green manure. The right crop for each situation will depend on environmental conditions, including soil moisture and temperature, as well as the particular reason for using a green manure crop.

A green manure crop must:
- suit the local soils and climate
- provide a large quantity of humus-forming material in the growing time available
- be able to compete with weeds.

A large root system is just as important and useful as a mass of aboveground growth. Many commonly recommended green manures have vigorous root systems that mine the soil for nutrients, open up or loosen the soil, encourage microbial life in the soil and produce large quantities of organic matter at depth in the soil when they die.

Legumes (nitrogen-fixing plants) and non-legumes are suitable for use as a green manure. A mixture of different species, including legumes and non-legumes, is also suitable and may return a better mix of nutrients to the soil.

Turning in

Green manures should generally be turned in while still green and actively growing, or before the crop reaches maturity and produces seed. If you are using non-legumes it may be necessary to supply a little additional nitrogen, in the form of composted manure or liquid compost, at the time of ploughing in to speed decomposition. Do not overcultivate (work the soil too much and destroy soil structure) when turning manure crops in.

Vegetable crops may be planted about three to six weeks later if conditions are ideal, or longer if the breakdown of the green manure is slowed by low temperature or insufficient moisture. Planting too early will damage tender young seedlings or transplants.

Chopping green manure before incorporating into the soil will help speed decomposition. Crops more than 20 centimetres tall can be slashed first, which may help to make turning in easier.

Do not turn green manures in too deeply because they should decompose rapidly in the presence of air. Anaerobic decomposition (lacking oxygen) may occur if it's buried too deep. The humus manufactured during anaerobic conditions may not last as long in the soil.

Select green manure species that do not regrow from the roots (such as most annuals) so they do not have to be turned in to the soil. Just cut them to the soil surface and let them form a mulch cover and eventually decompose. Even weeds can be used in this way to provide the benefits of green manure. This method will work even underneath trees, shrubs or vines.

Some green manures such as sorghum, Japanese millet (*Echinochloa esculenta*) and clover can be cut several times during their vegetative growth phase to increase production of organic matter. Mowing later in the growth cycle kills Japanese millet and sorghum, but clovers may need to be lightly tilled in.

Green manure in small gardens

Green manure crops take up space, but the benefits of green manure can still be obtained by more intimately integrating them into the garden. Selectively hand-pull weeds to allow self-germinating clovers to grow between larger plants, such as corn, and longer-growing plants, such as old varieties of brassica. Taller-growing plants can also be used, especially if they are cut regularly and used to mulch the main crop.

Spot planting

Plant green manure in any bare spots in the garden. Use peas, beans, clovers, ryegrass or any other fast-growing plants to fill vacant patches before weeds take hold. They can be left to grow tall and turned in, or cut and used as a regular supply of mulch material.

Some crops are well suited to polyculture growing systems. In a densely planted mixed species garden, the green manure can become a cover crop or 'living mulch', existing semi-permanently under the main crop. Clover or trefoil (*Trifolium* species) growing under corn, perhaps with inter-planted squash or melon (*Curcumis* species), is an example of a polyculture with an integrated green manure.

Great green manure crops

Legumes

- **Lupin** (*Lupinus* species) — Sow these legumes in the autumn
- **Lucerne** (*Medicago sativa*) — This perennial is very deep-rooted and persistent and is an excellent soil builder
- **Field peas** (*Pisum sativum*) — Sow from May through to early spring
- **Broad bean** (*Vicia faba*) — Also known as faba beans. Sow in autumn
- **Cowpea** (*Vigna unguiculata*) — Sow after frost until February
- **White clover** (*Trifolium repens*) — Sow in autumn

Non-legumes
- **Barley** (*Hordeum vulgare*) — Sow in autumn
- **Buckwheat** (*Fagopyrum esculentum*) — Sow in early summer
- **Japanese millet** (*Echinochloa esculenta*) — Sow from October to February
- **Millet** (family Poaceae) — Sow in late winter and spring
- **Mustard or kale** (*Brassica* species) — There are varieties to sow in spring or summer and autumn to winter
- **Oats** (*Avena* species) — Sow in autumn
- **Ryegrass** (*Lolium* species) — Sow in spring and autumn
- **Cereal rye** (*Secale cereale*) — Sow in late autumn
- **Sudan grass** (*Sorghum bicolor drummondi*) — Sow in late summer
- **Wheat** (*Triticum* species) — Sow in autumn

SMOTHER CROPS

A smother crop is a short-term crop grown to smother weeds. A typical smother crop in southern Australia would be vetch (*Vicia villosa*). In the north *Dolichos* species are used, as well as cowpea (*Vigna unguiculata*) or soybean (*Glycine max*). The strong-growing legumes ramble over other weeds and shade them out. The vetch itself could become a weed, but it will have more positive benefits (such as nitrogen fixation) and be easier to handle (it's susceptible to hoeing or hand-pulling) than the smothered weed.

A good thing about smother crops is you can use many edible species. Thickly sown flat-leaf parsley (*Petroselenium crispum* var. *neapolitanum*), spinach (*Spinacia oleracea*), silver beet (*Beta vulgaris*) and radish (*Raphanus sativus*) make excellent smother crops. Other possibilities include potato (*Solanum tuberosum*), cabbage and cauliflower (*Brassica oleracea*), beetroot (*Beta vulgaris*), turnip (*Brassica rapa*) and sweet potato (*Ipomoea batatas*).

Biennial and perennial vegetables can also be excellent smother crops, including globe artichoke (*Cynara scolymus*), Jerusalem artichoke (*Helianthus tuberosus*) and asparagus (*Asparagus officinalis*).

INTERCROPPING

Intercropping refers to the process of growing more than one crop in the same space to crowd out weeds. A good example is radish, fast-growing lettuce or spring onion grown between young cabbage, cauliflower or broccoli. The quick-growing spring crop of salad onion, lettuce or radish is harvested before the brassicas need the space. Fast-growing brassicas such as rocket and mustard are also good for filling any space in the garden. Any annual flowers or vegetables may also be grown in gaps as an herbaceous border.

Any cut-and-come-again salad crops make excellent intercrop plants — they stay low, fill the space, smother weeds and provide a good yield.

> **GREAT INTERCROP IDEAS**
> - Beans (*Phaseolus vulgaris*) with spinach (*Spinacia oleracea*)
> - Celery (*Apium graveolens*) with turnip (*Brassica rapa var. rapa*)
> - Broccoli (*Brassica oleracea*) with carrots (*Daucus carota*)

BARRIER PLANTINGS

An extension to the idea of cover crops is a weed invasion barrier consisting of very competitive plants that can stop weed seeds, runners and rhizomes. Depending on the situation, this could be trees and shrubs, such as *Casuarina* species (particularly good at stopping windblown seed), or dense groundcovers, such as cannas, agapanthus and iris, or ramblers, such as nasturtium. Cannas are my favourite in southern Australia for stopping invasive grasses such as couch.

Comfrey (*Symphytum officinale*) is sometimes recommended as a barrier planting, but it can be vigorously invasive. Be prepared to dig back a comfrey bed annually. Use the dug comfrey to make compost or liquid manure. Break up any large roots before adding to the compost heap.

Wormwood (*Artemisia absinthium*) makes a very good barrier. Plant it close or prune wider spaced plants to make them spread. They naturally make thick leaf mulch underneath that then releases alkaloids with an allelopathic effect. Cut the wormwood back regularly and use the pruned material to mulch problem weeds.

Barrier plantings can also include many edible fruits. Some suggestions for suitable species include plums (*Prunus* species), hazelnuts (*Corylus* species), guava (*Psidium* species), quince (*Cydonia oblonga*), loquat (*Eriobotrya japonica*), black passionfruit (*Passiflora edulis*), olives (*Olea europaea*) or other species that can be planted closely to form a hedgerow and are hardy to regular pruning back. But avoid species that are likely to become environmental weeds in your area, such as olives or banana passionfruit (*Passiflora millissima*).

Edible annual species can also be used as a temporary barrier planting. Leek and rocket are ideal species but anything that can be close-planted to achieve a complete smothering canopy is suitable.

TO MAKE LIQUID FERTILISER FROM WEEDS:

- Loosely fill a plastic rubbish bin or metal drum with weeds, fill with water and cover.
- Stir every two to four days.
- Leave to mature for at least two or three weeks, or until any pungent ammonium smells have disappeared.
- Filter the liquid and dilute with water at least three to one.
- Apply to plants or soil.
- The mixture can be reused by simply leaving the solids in the drum and topping up with water. After the second time, toss the old weeds into the compost.
- Will work best with freshly pulled weeds that have been actively growing.
- Small quantities of organic fertilisers, manure or liquid seaweed may be added to the brew.

Dense native shelterbelts (windbreaks) comprised of mixed trees, shrubs and groundcovers also protect from invasive weeds and provide a natural harbour for many beneficial organisms, especially predatory and parasitoid insects capable of controlling many garden pests. For maximum benefit, consult an indigenous vegetation expert in your district and select species that provide continuous sequential flowering. Such experts may include nursery or garden centre staff, members of the Society for Growing Australian Plants or Greening Australia and other conservation groups, or park rangers. Some Western Australian eucalypts are known for their high canopy and allelopathic effect on the understorey, which does not carry fire from the ground to the crown of the trees. They can be used to maintain a fire barrier around valuable assets.

GROUNDCOVERS

A more familiar idea than cover cropping is simply to plant areas with groundcover plants — species that are designed to grow prostrate or close to the ground. They also look appealing and add another dimension to the garden.

Cover crops may provide temporary plant cover for under-utilised areas or they may be more permanently established under other crop or garden plants. Groundcovers are designed to provide permanent or semi-permanent coverage and are generally selected primarily for their ornamental appeal. They are generally associated with low-maintenance gardens and certainly need less care than many other plants once they are established.

The precise definition of a groundcover plant varies, but usually groundcover plants have the following characteristics.

Groundcover plants:
- are perennial
- have a trailing, creeping or clumping growth habit
- are less than about 50 centimetres high.

Sometimes low shrubs growing to 1 metre are also included as groundcover plants. Groundcovers can be used to replace lawns and thereby reduce water use. Select groundcovers that are capable of making a complete canopy cover as soon as possible so that they become capable of shading out weeds.

Nurseries and garden centres also sell a range of short-lived plants as annual groundcovers. As these need to be replaced every year, they should offer some additional benefit, such as attractive flowers and foliage.

Remember that the groundcover plants themselves will need protection from weeds until they establish a canopy over the soil — that could be weeks for annuals, or months or years for perennials, depending on the type and size of the initial plant stock and planting density. Use an adequate depth of long-lasting mulch such as bark chips to protect the groundcovers for the first few seasons. Once established, the groundcovers listed below should be quite self-sufficient.

TIM'S TIPS FOR SELECTING GROUNDCOVERS

When setting out to buy groundcovers for your garden, select species that:

- are adapted to your district so that they have a reasonable chance of thriving in local conditions (soil, rainfall, temperature) and that they will be competitive against weeds with few inputs such as fertilisers
- are protective of the soil or will improve the nature of the soil
- are self-sufficient by way of pruning or other cultural activities
- will require little supplementary watering once established.

This list only represents a few favourite groundcovers that do have the capacity to out-compete weeds. They are reasonably self-sufficient once established and look attractive. Many other species are also suitable. Investigate public and private gardens, garden centres and nurseries in your area to discover the wonderful diversity of suitable groundcover plant types.

Groundcovers with weed-suppressing potential

Plant name	Habit	Ease of growing	Drought tolerance
Bellflower (*Campanula* species)	• About 300 species from 15–30 cm high	• Easy to grow by dividing the clumps	• Some species. Check with professional
Bugle (*Ajuga reptans*)	• Low growing plant; spreads from runners to form a dense mat	• Easy to grow from divisions of existing plants • Needs occasional grooming to remove dry flower stalks, etc.	• Low
Catnip (*Nepeta faassenii*)	• Wide-spreading, low growing evergreen	• Easy to grow from seed	• Medium
Spreading correa (*Correa decumbens*) and other *Correa* species	• Australian native with attractive bell flowers from 30–90 cm	• Easy to grow from cuttings	• High
Creeping boobialla (*Myoporum parvifolium*)	• Low growing shrub that also will climb a little or droop	• Easy to grow from cuttings	• High
Fan flower (*Scaevola aemula*) Also *Scaevola albida* or other *Scaevola* species	• Australian native; member of the Goodenaceae family • Many species and cultivars flowering from white to blue or purple	• Grows easily from seed or cuttings	• High
Feverfew (*Chrysanthemum parthenium*)	• 30–90 cm, depending on variety and location	• Easy to grow from seed	• Medium

Sun	Shade	Comments
• Tolerates sun for part of the day	• Prefers light shade	• Attractive blue flowers • Prefers good drainage
• Will grow in the sun in cool locations. Use variegated varieties in sunny spots	• Prefers light shade	• Showy flowers for moist shady sites • Excellent under trees
• Sun or shade	• Sun or shade	• May attract cats
• Sun-loving	• Some varieties or other *Correa* species can handle shade	• Attractive, drooping bell flowers
• Sun or shade	• Sun or shade	• Hardy • Flowers will attract birds • Will handle clay and saline soils
• Sun-loving	• Light shade	• Prefers good drainage • Some species or cultivars grow well in a range of soils, many are well suited to sandy areas
• Can handle full sun in most locations	• Will tolerate partial shade	• Some weediness potential in certain areas

Plant name	Habit	Ease of growing	Drought tolerance
Gazania (*Gazania* species)	• Low growing, spreading	• Very easy from seed or transplants	• High
Geranium (*Geranium* species)	• Hardy; low maintenance	• Grows well from cuttings	• Medium
Geranium ivy (*Pelargonium peltatum*)	• Evergreen; grows to 30–60 cm	• Easy to grow	• Medium
Grevillea (*Grevillea* species)	• Australian native; many forms from prostrate shrubs to tall trees	• Easy to grow	• Medium
Ivy (*Hedera* species) English ivy (*H. Helix*)	• Hardy; low maintenance; dwarf and large-leaf forms • Stop it from climbing up things and it will seed much less.	• Easy to grow even in poor soils • Trim edges three or four times per year	• Medium
Juniper (*Juniperus communis*) *Juniperus* species (*J. horizontalis*)	• Evergreen with blue, silver or bronze tints • Many species with great height range but many prostrate forms	• Easy to grow once established • Consider using advanced plants to cover large areas	• High
Lambs ear (*Stachys byzantina*)	• Hardy; low maintenance evergreen	• Easy to grow; low care	• Medium
Phlox (*Phlox subulata*)	• Spreading growth to 15 cm	• Easily grown and propagated	• Low

Sun	Shade	Comments
• Sun-loving	• Prefers sunny position	• Good colour display from daisy-type flowers for long periods in frost-free areas. • Weed potential adjacent to bushland
• Sun or partial shade	• Sun or partial shade	• Geranium may be hardier than pelargonium
• Sun or shade	• Sun or shade	• Does not like frost
• Sun or partial shade	• Prefers sunny position	• Flowers will attract birds
• Tolerates full sun except in very hot areas	• Tolerates deep shade	• Dependable. Will stabilise steep banks • Dwarf ivy varieties combine well with bulbs • Sometimes the rapid easy growth of ivy can be a setback as it harbours pests (blackbirds, slugs) and will climb and damage structures
• Sun-loving	• Tolerates some shade but foliage colour may become dull	• Dependable and practical groundcovers
• Grey–silver foliage makes this plant sun-hardy	• Prefers sunny position and handles afternoon sun in hot locations	• Kids love the thick felt-like leaves
• Sun-loving	• Prefers full sun	• Mass of small pink, white, red or blue flowers when in bloom • Prefers well-drained soil

Plant name	Habit	Ease of growing	Drought tolerance
Pigface (*Carpobrotus* species)	• Australian native succulent	• Easily grown and propagated by cuttings	• High
Pinks (*Dianthus* species)	• Hardy perennial to 15 cm • 300 species	• Easy to grow once established	• Low
Rock rose (*Cistus* species)	• Low evergreen shrub	• Easy to grow • Requires occasional pruning	• High
Rosemary (*Rosmarinus officinalis*)	• Evergreen shrub to 2 m, but low growing cultivars are available	• Easy to grow; pinch tips to encourage spreading • Will handle heavy pruning	• Medium
Sedum (*Sedum* species) Jellybean plant (*S. rubrotinctum*) Stonecrop (*S. spectabile*)	• Succulent; grows 15–29 cm with sprawling stems • Many different forms	• Grows easily from cuttings	• High
Thyme (*Thymus* species)	• Hardy perennial to 20 cm high • 300 species	• Easy to grow from rooted sections, tip cuttings and seed	• Medium
Native violet (*Viola hederacea*)	• Australian native spreading plant to 15 cm	• Easy to grow	• Low or nil
Woody yarrow (*Achillea tomentosa*)	• Evergreen	• Easy to grow	• Medium

Sun	Shade	Comments
• Sun-loving	• Prefers full sun	• Very hardy to exposed conditions including windy and coastal locations
• Sun-loving	• Prefers full sun	• Showy white-and-red flowers and grey–green leaves. • Soil must be well drained
• Prefers sunny position	• Sun-loving	• Good flower display tolerates hot exposed sites
• Prefers sunny position	• Sun-loving	• Use leaves and twigs in the kitchen
• Sun-loving	• Tolerates some shade but foliage colour may become dull	• Jellybean plant is also called stonecrop — leaves turn red–bronze in full sunlight • *Spectabile* has bright red autumn flowers • Many other species also make suitable groundcovers • Prefers occasional drought and handle poor soil
• Sun-loving	• Prefers sunny position	• Needs well-drained soil • Grows in poor soil • Mother of thyme or woolly thyme are excellent for use between flagstones • Use thyme in the kitchen
• Sun-loving	• Will handle semi-shade	• Will tolerate some foot traffic
• Sun-loving	• Will handle partial shade	• Hardy

PHYSICAL AND MECHANICAL METHODS
Trenching and solid barriers

A trench 50 centimetres deep and 15 centimetres wide will stop all but the most invasive weeds such as horsetail (*Equisetium* species) and some bamboos (*Bambusa* species) from entering a garden. If it's not safe to leave a trench open, you can try inserting a vertical barrier such as thick polythene (the type used by builders underneath foundations) but the barrier will need to be continuous to stop perennials such as couch and kikuyu. Be sure to use plenty of overlap when laying non-continuous sheets. Weeds such as couch and kikuyu may also grow over the barrier at the soil surface, so continual maintenance of the boundary is required.

Germination barriers
Mulch

Mulch is most often organic (plant based) in origin but it works in a physical way to impede the germination and growth of weeds, chiefly by restricting light, which is the trigger for germination in many species. Mulch will form a barrier to small germinating seeds or underground plant parts that are trying to reach the light.

Germination in different plant types may be triggered by various events including temperature changes and sunlight. Many plants use exposure to sunlight as a clue to germinate and this in part explains why cultivation results in production of a new generation of weeds.

Mulch needs regular maintenance, including topping it up as it breaks down and pulling out any weeds that do appear. If weeds are growing only in the mulch layer they should pull out easily. Mulch will also keep the soil underneath in good condition so that even weeds rooted in the soil should be easy to pull.

Mulch is often an adequate technique for the control of annual weeds, but may not stop aggressive perennial weeds that grow from runners.

Mulch also moderates soil temperature. It will keep soil cool in summer, reduce evaporation from the soil surface and keep plants productive longer. For instance, mulched zucchini or button squash will produce fruit later into the season and broccoli will continue producing side shoots, whereas unmulched plants may bolt to seed. Earthworms and other soil organisms are encouraged and stay active longer under mulch, and they remain closer to the vital feeder roots near the soil surface. Mulch will raise crop yield and improve plant health by retaining advantageous organisms and providing a beneficial effect on the soil.

In winter and early spring in southern Australia it may be necessary to pull mulch back to keep soil warm. Used in conjunction with drip irrigation, mulch can significantly reduce water use.

Mulch is best suited to longer-lived plants but can also be used with short-lived vegetables and flowers. Natural mulch also adds organic matter to the soil. Because mulch keeps leaves and flowers clean by reducing rain splash, there are fewer opportunities to spread soil-borne diseases.

Mulch will save you and the community money by reducing landfill, water bills, fertiliser requirements and — if you grow your own — food and cut-flower bills.

Organic mulch materials

Animal manures have some nutrient value but they must be well aged and preferably well composted, otherwise they can add weed seeds and provide too much readily available nitrogen for many situations.

Paper is a suitable mulch for a number of reasons: it stops light reaching the soil surface; it's easy to apply; it makes a great worm highway at the soil surface underneath the paper layer; it eventually breaks down to organic matter; and it keeps some produce such as strawberries and lettuce very clean.

There are many ways to use paper, including the following:

- sheets of newspaper or cardboard are spread on the ground and covered with other organic material such as straw or leaves. Use paper at least a dozen sheets thick and overlap the paper to provide a continuous barrier to germination. The other mulch material keeps the paper in place
- shredded paper (available from offices) makes a fine mulch material. It mats down quickly once wetted and does not blow easily like uncovered newspaper
- flattened cardboard boxes make a suitable mulch, but it is best to avoid waxed boxes and to remove non-organic packing tape that may have been used to seal the box. Edges can be buried in a shallow trench to stop them blowing away and to prevent weeds from emerging from under the layer. Be aware: the buried section will deteriorate rapidly.

> In the past, some gardening books recommended avoiding newsprint because it contained toxic inks. This information is out of date and all inks used now are vegetable-based and safe for compost or garden use. Avoid glossy paper.

Leaves from deciduous trees, such as oaks, and **pine needles** will gradually acidify the soil. Use them where soil pH needs adjustment and under crops that appreciate acid conditions, such as strawberries.

Grass clippings need care as they may contain seeds or even pieces of couch that could grow. They should also not be used in thick layers as they mat down, staying very wet and restricting air movement into soil. About 5 to 10 centimetres is enough. Lawn clippings are best mixed with other materials or converted to compost before use. Let clippings dry before using as mulch, to stop nodes from producing roots.

Compost should be weed-free. It makes excellent mulch for sites where the soil needs improving, especially on vegetable beds. If compost is exposed to bright sunshine it should be protected with a layer of less valuable mulch on the top. Sawdust, seaweed or straw are ideal for covering compost.

Straw is a popular mulch material that has been used by gardeners for years. So-called white straw, or cereal straw, is longer lasting than pea straw or lucerne, but these products contribute some nitrogen to the soil. Meadow hay should generally be avoided for mulching because it's likely to have a greater risk of weed seeds. The price of whole bales has increased over the past few years because of the ongoing drought, and agricultural technology has moved to very large round or square bales unsuitable for garden use. However, chopped straw products, including sugarcane mulch, are now readily available substitutes.

About 3 to 5 centimetres of straw provides very useful mulch. Organic mulches such as straw, particularly when used at this depth, will prevent many small seeds from germinating, both by excluding light and by providing a significant barrier

TIM'S STRAW MULCH TECHNIQUE

I use multiple layers of newspaper under straw mulch, but novices should pay careful attention to soil moisture levels. Soil must be thoroughly soaked before the paper layer is added, as the mulch can absorb significant quantities of water before the soil begins to rewet. The technique remains a very useful one, but possibly unsuitable for sprinkler application of water. Use drippers or watering cans to deliver water directly to the root zone of the crop plants.

to emergence of young seedlings. Seeds may germinate within the mulch layer itself, but these will be easily pulled from the loose mulch. The mulch improves friability of the soil surface, making of any plants with larger seeds that do manage to get through the mulch layer much easier to remove.

Seaweed is excellent mulch material. However, avoid it (or mix with other materials) if you have salty soils and low rainfall. Don't waste water trying to wash salt off seaweed because most of the salt is inside the tissues. Seaweed will introduce micronutrients to the soil and is a great mulch if you have free-draining soils and high rainfall.

Bagasse is the dry pulpy residue left after the processing of sugarcane. It is available from sugar mills or in bags from garden centres. It is slow to break down but it may contain pesticide residues, so it's better suited to use on ornamentals than vegetables. Bagasse can become compacted, so mix it with coarser materials.

Mushroom compost is available from mushroom farms or garden centres. Pile the compost and let it reheat for two to six weeks before using. It quickly turns into a very dark-coloured and fine-textured material. Mushroom compost generally does not last very long and it may be alkaline, so is best suited to annual plants (adjust the pH by sprinkling soil with elemental sulphur before using on rhododendrons, camellias or other acid-loving plants) or to mixing with longer-lasting materials.

Mushroom compost is less valuable than homemade or good commercial compost and it may contain non-organic residues. It is best to order mushroom compost four to six weeks before it is needed and re-compost it prior to use. This is most important if it will be incorporated into soil — and less critical if only used on the soil surface.

Weeds are freely available and contain many useful nutrients. The downside is that they may also contain seeds. Pull weeds before they set seed whenever possible. They may not be the most attractive mulch, but will provide some benefits. Try to avoid nutgrass, oxalis and other noxious weeds.

A variety of other materials is suitable for mulching. Availability will vary depending on where you live, but possibilities include rice hulls, shredded cane grass, grape marc, almond shells and husk, sawdust or other processing waste.

Minerals such as gravel, scoria or pebbles, brown coal and other forms of stone are suitable mulches but they are best placed over the top of weed-barrier fabrics. Although small weeds may germinate, they are easily pulled from the loose gravel. Minerals can be used to add colour and texture to a garden and are particularly well suited to cacti and succulent gardens. Flame weeding with a small hand-held gas wand is an excellent technique for gravel mulch or paths.

Shell is also suitable if you can find quantities from a shelly beach or an oyster processor. Seek local council approval before removing large quantities of shell from the beach.

Mad for mulch

The advantages of mulch
There's no tillage Less digging means less hard work. You preserve the soil structure because you're not lifting and turning the soil. Mulch also creates a perfect environment for worms.

Soil cover is better Mulched soil stays cooler in summer, reduces evaporation and saves soil water. It also reduces soil compaction from rainfall, heavy watering and foot traffic.

There's no waiting You don't have to wait before planting if organic materials are only added at the soil surface, unless they are strongly allelopathic or growth inhibiting. If organic matter other than well-finished compost is incorporated, it's advisable to wait at least six weeks for the materials to break down before planting because nitrogen will be tied up by the decomposer organisms. Phytotoxic chemicals released during this decomposition may retard plant growth.

Soil structure improves The influence of the mulch is extended down into the soil because moisture from rainfall is retained, earthworms and other animals are sheltered and these effects eventually create an excellent soil structure. The soil will be loose and no digging will be required other than small holes for planting seedlings.

The disadvantages of mulch

There is a potential for contamination When new materials are introduced to the garden, there is a risk of introducing new weed seeds, pests and diseases. Mulch is responsible for the introduction of millipedes, snails and harlequin bugs into many gardens.

Soil may not warm Thick mulch will prevent soil from warming early in spring by stopping the heat of the sun from reaching soil. This can mean later planting or 'take off' of plants.

It's unsuitable for certain plants Mulching plants that grow from rhizomes and stolons can make vigorous weeds that grow from underground parts even stronger and harder to control at first.

It may reduce infiltration from light rainfall Mulches that absorb a lot of water can reduce the effectiveness of light rainfall or irrigation.

Avoiding the disadvantages

You can avoid the potential problems from mulching if you follow these few suggestions:

Use care when selecting mulch materials Locate good sources of organic fertilisers, clean well-made compost and organic or spray-free organic material. Use straw rather than hay, because there's usually less weed seed in straw.

Keep mulch away from plant stems Keeping the mulch pulled back will minimise the risk of collar rot.

Use drip irrigation Install drip irrigation under mulch and leave small unmulched areas around plants. Disturb mulch with a fork or rake it back during showers to encourage penetration of rainwater. Irrigate less often, but for longer periods, or avoid mulches with very high water-holding potential, such as straw. Adjust your irrigation practices to accommodate the absorption capacity of the mulch material itself, such as using fewer but longer irrigations or placing drip lines underneath. The water that reaches the soil will be conserved, leading to a net benefit.

Use simple barriers around young seedlings Use plastic containers with the bottoms removed, or gauze covers to exclude snails, slugs and other pests.

Pull mulch back in early spring to warm the soil Old mulch may be composted or loosely stacked and replaced when the soil is warm again.

Control difficult weeds first Try to get weeds such as couch grass under control before applying the mulch. Thick mulch may stop small bits of root or rhizome from growing whereas larger pieces will grow through the mulch.

Mulch is a must

Good organic mulch is the best thing you can do for your garden. Almost any plant material can be used, although some will last a shorter or longer time, some will be more nutritious, or will have other desirable properties, such as colour to match the landscape setting.

Some of the benefits of mulch, such as protection of the soil surface, apply to almost any organic material used. It is possible to maximise the number of benefits obtained by selecting mulch materials that serve several functions.

How much mulch?

Woody perennial plants and strong-growing erect annuals can handle a greater depth of mulch. The actual depth of mulch used also depends upon the type of weeds you want to stop and availability of mulching material.

Deep mulch can be up to 20 centimetres of loose organic waste, such as weed-free straw.

Finer mulches, including grass clippings and compost, need to be used in a thinner layer because they are likely to compact down further and may cause water to run off before penetrating soil. A depth of 5 centimetres should be enough.

Weed-proof fabrics

Biodegradable films are made from a variety of materials (principally natural starch) and are currently making good headway in Europe, for both professional and home garden use. At least one European company has visited Australia to assess the market for these products. Generally, they are used in the same way as paper and cardboard mulch.

Weed-proof fabrics make a complete barrier to weed growth. Only starch-based biodegradable film or woven polypropylene fabrics are permitted in organic growing. Woven fabrics allow movement of air and water into the soil. There are also non-woven permeable products that are acceptable.

Weed-proof fabrics are different to geo-fabrics, which are generally designed to encourage soil stability and to encourage germination and growth of plants through the fabric. Fabrics are not effective for standing weeds, and existing weeds must be removed before laying the weed barrier. They are ideal for use under gravel or bark. Make sure you cut planting holes through the fabric with a sharp knife.

Fabrics can be purchased in sheets, off the roll, or in pre-cut planting patches in various shapes and sizes. Planting holes may need attention to remove seedlings and runners that germinate close to the plant.

I have never found the use of carpet to be satisfactory, mainly because they are too hard to remove when they deteriorate and they may be impregnated with long-lasting chemicals. Some carpet underfelts even contain asbestos fibres. There may be a

MULCH TIMING

Mulch is best applied when the soil is warm and moist. Too wet and it may take a long time to dry out. Too dry and it may prevent soil from wetting enough because the mulch itself holds back moisture.

use for woollen carpets but my advice would be to avoid synthetic ones altogether.

Individual plant mulch mats can be purchased in different sizes and shapes. They can be made from coir, jute, wool, paper, cardboard, woven polypropylene or other suitable materials and combine well with a surface covering of bark, wood chip or gravel and pebble.

Light restriction

Weeds need access to light and therefore restricting access helps to reduce the competitiveness of newly germinated weed seedlings. This can be done with mulch or by using close planting distances between and within the row. Close planting can be much more successful in a polyculture than a monoculture situation, especially when you are using proven plant 'guilds', such as sweet corn, beans and squash. Some crops, such as onion or garlic, will never establish enough canopy when planted alone, but they can be mixed with a leafier crop such as celery to provide better surface cover. Leeks will develop a canopy and benefit from close planting because they produce long stalks. Cylindrical beetroot produces a long root that grows well above the soil surface and it will also form a dense canopy if planted close together.

TOUGH PERENNIAL WEEDS

For really tough perennial weed problems use thick, long-lasting mulch such as woollen carpet, cardboard with a topping of other organic matter (compost, straw, seaweed, etc.) or permeable plastic.

Very little intense light is required to stimulate seeds to germinate. Light does not penetrate far into soil, although some level of light will exist a few centimetres down. All it may take is exposing a buried seed to less than a second of bright sunlight when soil is turned over by digging and it can germinate. Experimental proof of this has lead European organic producers to fashion laser-guided ploughing systems so that they can plough at night without headlights on the tractor. They plough in darkness because even ploughing on the full moon with a clear sky will stimulate more germination than a dark night. This might take some effort to replicate in the home garden!

> ### When the mulch is finished
>
> Organic mulch will eventually thin out because a lot of it has been slowly incorporated into the soil. You may also need to clear mulch away in order to establish small-seeded crops such as carrots or parsley. At this point, it's best to rake it off and take it away to the compost heap, or to another bed where it can be used as mulch.
>
> If you dig the remaining mulch into the soil it will cause an increase in the population of soil organisms that break the organic matter down, and the organisms will temporarily capture nitrogen from the soil for their own growth. You will need to wait four to six weeks before planting, depending on the temperature (decomposition in cold soils takes longer).

WATER MANAGEMENT
Water restriction
Weeds grow where the resources of sunlight, nutrients and water are available to them. Restricting these resources, particularly water, by applying it directly to the root zone of the desirable plants can significantly limit weed growth. Techniques such as watering

cans, buried water systems (leaky tape) or drippers are much more accurate for the application of irrigation water. Micro-sprinklers are better than butterfly or impact sprinklers at directing water to the crop plant and restricting the wetted zone where weeds can grow.

Temporary flooding

Some of my friends are organic cereal and rice farmers and they are fortunate in that virtually all their weed problems are susceptible to either cultivation or their system of flooding temporary bays to fill the subsoil with moisture. This is hard to replicate in the home garden, but you can submerge weed-infested pots in a bucket of water to get rid of shallow rooted weeds, such as chickweed and rosette-stage biennials.

Drainage

Low-lying and poorly drained areas may encourage weeds such as sedges (*Cyperus* species) and rushes (*Juncus* species), cumbungi (*Typha* species), common reeds (*Phragmites communis*) and water hyacinth (*Eichhornia crassipes*). Improving drainage will help to control these weeds.

Shade and high soil moisture together may encourage weeds such as pennywort (*Hydrocotyl umbellate)* or pearlwort (*Sagina procumbens*).

If developing a flooded area, try planting water chestnuts (*Eleocharis dulcis*) a year in advance. When you dig over the wet area, harvest the nuts as a bonus reward from digging.

NUTRIENT MANIPULATION

Weeds will always be with us, but the particular suite of weeds that survives in a place is the result of historical exposure, weed-control effort and the environmental conditions that favour a particular weed over its competitors, including other weeds. As a result, the particular weeds that gain prominence over time are at least in part a response to soil conditions. If we understand this, we can use the knowledge in two ways.

Firstly, the weeds (or for that matter the native plants) that grow in a place can be used as indicators of soil condition. This may then provide a clue to how to treat the weed.

In the past, it was this type of approach that was labelled 'offbeat' and 'unscientific' by reductionists. It was never unscientific; it in fact makes a great deal of sense. It's common knowledge where I live that the change in species from stringy bark to box eucalypts is often associated with the different geology of a place and therefore the different soil type and nutrient conditions. It is even possible to go prospecting for metal with a little plant knowledge. Visit any copper-mining town and you may see among the most prominent weeds a plant called tree tobacco (*Nicotiana glauca*) because it copes well in soils with very high copper levels.

Acquiring this knowledge is not straightforward, but many indigenous species experts, field geologists, research soil scientists and alert farmers have it. Many farmers recognise that their weeds change subtly with soil type, but most have not translated this into their weed management program. Three interesting books dealing with organic weed control provide particularly useful information on this topic: *Weeds and What They Tell* by Ehrenphried Pfeiffer (1981, Oregon); *Weeds: Guardians of the Soil* by Joseph A. Cocannouer (1950, Old Greenwich, Connecticut); and *Weeds: Control Without Poisons* by Charles Walters (1991, Austin, Texas). Read with caution, though, because these books were written for the northern hemisphere, where there are different soils, and the common names of weeds will sometimes denote different species. It's necessary to acquire local knowledge and to develop your powers of observation — a useful skill for organic growers.

Case study: know your area

In the Mount Lofty Ranges, where I live, many pastures have low-pH (acidic) soils that are prone to capeweed. Some people use herbicides to control it and they become good clients of the herbicide retailer, mainly because the capeweed comes back again every year. It isn't really hard to get rid of capeweed in my region, in fact — all you do is spread some dolomite. This doesn't mean that you will never see a capeweed plant again, but there will be fewer and the population will not thrive as it does in untreated soils.

Get to know your region. Speak to neighbours, especially if they've lived in the area for a long time, and ask their advice. A little local knowledge goes a long way.

Here are a few other things I've learned along the way:
- if weedy grasses are dominant, try improving calcium availability by adding calcium
- if broadleaf weeds dominate, adjust the ratio of phosphate to potassium. A suitable balance is 2:1 for vegetables and 4:1 for lawns or pasture
- some books recommend sulphate of ammonia for weeds such as bindii or oxalis but I don't consider this an organic technique. I would instead recommend mulching with fruit pumice. Keen organic gardeners sometimes save their urine for this purpose also. Keep it for at least several days to 'mature' it before using.

Keep plants growing

Nutrient supply is also critical in keeping garden or crop plants growing vigorously so that they can compete well for light, water and space. Of course, optimum growing conditions for the plant are not only about nutrients or any other single factor; they are about overall plant health including selection of appropriate species and variety, water management, quarantine from serious pests or pathogens, and soil moisture.

PHYSICAL CONTROL
Hand-pulling

When I weed by hand, I tend to be very thorough but also very selective. I turn the pulled weeds into fine compost or mulch. Depending on the target weed, and where it is growing, I can work surprisingly quickly too.

KNOW YOUR SOIL BY THE WEEDS

Weeds commonly found in acid soils
- Buttercup (*Ranunculus repens*)
- Dock (*Rumex* species)
- Stinging nettles (*Urtica urens*)

Weeds commonly found in alkaline soils
- Chickweed (*Stellaria media*)
- Cleavers (*Galium aparine*)
- Fumitory (*Fumaria* species)

Weeds commonly found in compacted ground
- Wireweed (*Polygonum aviculare*)
- Guildford grass (*Romulea rosea*)

I like to be selective so that I can allow a certain suite of weeds to develop to maturity. In time, selective weeding will change the pattern of weeds to the species I prefer to deal with. These preferred weeds serve various functions in the garden, such as soil protection, nutrient sequestering, encouraging beneficial insects and smothering other weeds.

I like to leave some legumes, such as clovers and vetch (although they both take over and may need some thinning), as well as some edible herbs that also add to the flowering diversity and therefore encourage beneficial insects. I'll also leave some 'softer' weeds that can become a self-sown, endlessly renewable cover crop and green manure. By 'softer' weeds I mean those that fulfil their essential role of protecting the soil through significant growth, but are also easily pulled out. Such weeds take little horsepower to mow and easily release their grip on the soil when pulled.

I might use these weeds as green manure, by mowing or brush-cutting them to the ground and leaving them in place, or I might cart them away to the compost heap. As an avid composter, I've learned that once I get the worst weeds out of the way, there is a wonderful synchronicity between composting and weeding. I cart barrowloads of weeds off to the compost and return the finished compost to the soil. After continuous compost applications, the soil becomes soft and friable and the weeds are more easily pulled out, roots and all.

Other weeds that I allow in certain areas because I consider them easy to control include fumitory (*Fumaria* species), fat hen (*Chenopodium album*), cleavers (*Galium aparine*), pigweed (*Portulaca oleracea)*, sow thistle (*Sonchus oleraceus*) and plantain (*Plantago* species).

How to hand-weed efficiently and effectively:

- work within your physical and personal safety limits. Half an hour, once or twice a day, or even 10 minutes at a time, can achieve a great deal with a planned approach and some careful attention to the task
- try to schedule weeding when soil moisture is naturally high. If necessary, water the area the day before
- dress comfortably. Also consider safety, such as the need for overalls, boots and gloves
- use kneeling mats or tilers' kneepads for longer weeding sessions
- work from the edge of an infestation. Try to work in a line, removing as many weeds as possible
- try to ignore fleeing wildlife such as wolf spiders. They will almost always run away. Just move away from large spiders or other scary bugs
- if hand-pulling, grip the weed firmly as close to the soil surface as possible. Wiggle it a little and gently tug on it to see if it's loose. If there is little resistance, pull the

weed out of the soil. If you can grasp the crown root, just at or below the soil surface, there is much less chance that the weed will break than when gripping the top. After a few attempts you should be able to judge whether the weed will come free or will need a probe with a weeding tool

- a trowel is the universal hand-digging tool, but any long narrow tool will do. Many experienced gardeners will have a favourite tool, such as a flat screwdriver or small paint scraper, or a commercial tool such as a dandelion or dock digger. If digging tap-rooted plants such as dandelion, insert the tool as deeply as you can next to the base of the stem and wiggle the tool to loosen the soil immediately around the root
- shake the excess soil off the roots, but cut off the seed heads *before* digging. Weeds may be well adapted to dry conditions and are capable of regrowing. Even if they do not regrow, there may be enough moisture in the soil, roots and stem to sustain the weed long enough for seeds to mature on the pulled plant, especially in rainy or humid weather. African daisy will do this so readily that any thick succulent stems should be broken into pieces
- working within your limits, try to give the job a chance to work by keeping at it. Work over a few days, or several times a day, to make some progress
- regular is always better than spasmodic
- follow up your work and keep on top of regrowing weeds
- use the space you have reclaimed. Bare ground is an invitation for weeds to reinvade. If you can't plant something immediately, sow a cover crop or lay mulch to protect the soil and stop weeds from germinating.

There are many different ways of weeding depending on the soil condition and weed type. Another useful action is to slice just under the soil with an old kitchen knife or paint scraper, working the tool back and forth to sever roots. Pull the detached seedling tops from the soil and compost them or leave on the soil surface as a mulch.

If possible, remove any maturing seed heads with secateurs prior to pulling.

Finger and thumb grip on seedling

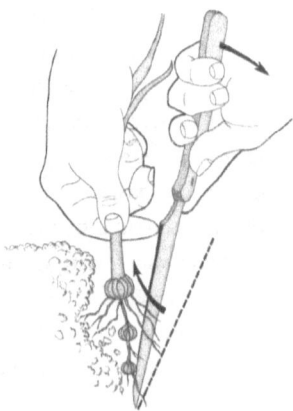

Use a kitchen knife to loosen soil

> ## Dave Duncan's weed replacement therapy
>
> **Dave Duncan** is an expert 'weedologist' with extensive experience of garden and environmental weeds in Queensland, South Australia and the desert country. He refers to his 'weed replacement therapy' and sometimes calls it the 'pull a weed, plant a seed' weed-control tactic. Dave keeps packets of seed close at hand, usually productive plants like parsley, rocket and lettuce, broccoli or pumpkin. He says, 'Let your vegetables be the weeds.' Self-seeding vegetables have now replaced the original weeds in Dave's garden.
>
> I agree — in fact, my self-sown tomatoes and pumpkins from the compost (they are two plants with seeds that will survive a hot compost) are often the best that I will grow that year.

Hand-digging for difficult weeds

A difficult weed such as soursob (*Oxalis pes-caprae*) is hard to remove by hand. Oxalis produces both tubers and bulbils, and successive generations of bulbs in the same spot pull themselves deeper into the soil.

Thoroughness and consistency are important if you want to successfully hand-pull soursob. Try these tips:

- always work from an edge. Create an edge if you must, but then work consistently forwards
- adequate soil moisture is critical for success. Try to schedule weeding when the soil is at field capacity (full of water), which probably means a few hours or days after rain. You can water small areas the day before if necessary
- take as much of the plant as possible, including as many bulbils as you can find. Pulling is much more effective than

mowing for weeds such as soursob because it removes more photosynthetic material and also more roots. Nutrients and water in the stems and roots left in the ground may be reacquired by the bulb and used to support the next attempt at growth. Taking more biomass away from the weed will make it weaker and slow its recovery. Remember to grip firmly and as low as you possibly can

- pull vertically. Be prepared to follow any natural fractures line in the soil, but if there is no direct advantage in doing it, try to pull straight up. Even if you leave the main bulb or some bulbils behind, at least you have pulled them closer to the surface so they are easier to get next time
- revisit several times to follow up. The sooner you get back the better, as long as there is some regrowth to latch onto. It is rarely possible to get everything in one pass, although in good soil conditions weeds will come away much more readily
- when the soursob is severely weakened, grow a quick smother crop of vetch or thickly sown parsley.

The worst situation is where soursob is growing through a thick root mat from trees or garden plants. Bulbs and bulbils will snag on the roots and detach from the plant. Regrowth will be severe and the only solution is to revisit frequently, still following the scheme outlined above. Any bulbs or tubers left behind must be weakened to the point of exhaustion. Bulbils may only have the reserves to grow once if they are deep in the soil, whereas mature bulbs may regrow many times before they give up.

There will probably be a time of the year when a large percentage of the old soursob bulbs have expended their energy. This time is called 'bulb exhaustion' stage and it's a good time to target weed control. The time varies across the country, but dig investigative holes until you notice the larger old bulbs becoming empty and flaky to the feel.

Notwithstanding bulb exhaustion, one central rule of soursob control remains. Control is always more successful before flowering. Small bulbs have already been produced once the flower appears.

Another way to limit soursob is to grow potatoes the season before. Dig individual small holes and plant potatoes. When the potatoes are ready, dig the entire bed, removing the potatoes, soursob and any other weeds.

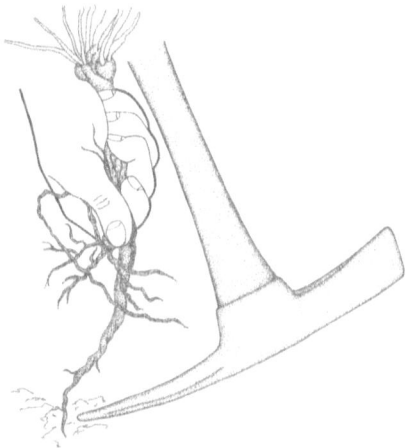

Use a mattock for larger roots or rhizomes

Just pulling tops of soursob, flaming or mowing it may slow it down a little, but it has significant reserves in underground bulbs and can come back quickly and often. There may be some considerable value in doing that, if you will eventually get to a more concerted control. Otherwise, save your energy and learn to appreciate the value of soursob as a weed. At least it adds colour and it dies away in summer. Organic grape growers in Willunga, South Australia, such as Joch Bosworth and Adrian Strachan, use soursob under their vines because it provides a dense groundcover during winter, naturally dies down to form a mulch over summer (and therefore does not compete for water) and comes back in the following autumn. In fact, they have converted a weed into an ideal cover crop for that difficult area down the row underneath the vine canopy and in the immediate vicinity of

Use weeds for compost or liquid fertiliser

Almost all weeds can go into the compost. Weeds that regrow from rhizomes or runners, such as couch, can be left on the soil surface to dry out. Sometimes, I use the shed roof or some spare sheets of roofing iron for this purpose — a concrete path is also fine. Put really aggressive weeds into a plastic bag for several weeks. Weeds that grow from large tubers may need to be kept longer before adding to the heap. Break the tubers up to speed drying time. It should only be necessary to dump or burn the most persistent parts, for example watsonia corms.

You can make liquid fertiliser from weeds using the following method:

1. Almost fill a plastic garbage bin or pickle barrel with freshly pulled weeds.
2. Cover the weeds with water and replace the lid.
3. You can also add small amounts of other garden products such as seaweed, fish emulsion, crushed basalt rock or organic fertiliser.
4. Stir the mixture occasionally.
5. Leave for several weeks, at least until any acrid ammonia smell has disappeared.
6. Dilute with water to the colour of weak tea (about 10:1) and pour over garden plants and soil.

the dripper system. Some effort is still required to keep it from spreading into the inter-row, where a diversity of other vegetation performs multiple functions. The inter-row is managed by mowing and sometimes re-sowing green manures and permanent sward.

Effective hand-weeding

There may be a compromise between being really effective with hand-weeding and the time spent on the job. To remove every last weed takes time, whereas a two-handed grab approach will clear an area fast.

It all depends on your goal. Slow and steady wins the race, so they say. Fast and furious will get the garden looking neat for that important social event, but if you really want to eliminate weeds from a particular area you must remove seed heads and slow down photosynthesis and therefore overall weed growth. There is a role for each of these strategies; the point is to know what your goals are and to work in the best possible way towards achieving them.

> I recently set out to consider why many of my colleagues advocated adding much more soil (and especially clay) to compost heaps than I did. After some observation of others and bit of forensic investigation of some buckets of pulled weeds in my garden, I discovered that I have been adding much more soil to my compost heaps than I realised.
>
> I always thought it was really good to leave some soil clinging to the roots of weeds before adding to the compost, as this will introduce a wide variety of soil organisms. After dissecting the results of some hand-weeding, I found that I could have up to 15 and even 20 per cent soil by weight.

Some people just squat while others prefer to kneel. Kneepads or a kneeling pad make it possible to spend longer on your knees. Becoming a really fast and effective weeder requires developing the ability to pluck or pull with both hands.

Cultivation

Clean cultivation (maintaining a totally weed-free soil surface) is rarely the preferred treatment for weeds, because it disturbs the natural soil profile, burns up (oxidises) organic matter, brings new weed seed to the soil surface and creates bare soil — an invitation to the next generation of weeds to germinate. However, cultivation in some form or another is frequently useful, particularly very shallow cultivation or 'surface tickle' used to dislodge small weed seedlings from the soil without the negative effects of deep digging. Digging of soursob (*Oxalis pes-caprae*), for instance, need not involve significant turnover of soil. The soil is loosened up, the weeds are pulled out from the loose soil and the soil is allowed to fall back into place with the least possible disturbance. Selective digging is best.

Hoeing is a form of cultivation. We use a rotary hoe to completely turn soil over; however, when cultivating friable bare soil, say between rows of recently planted vegetables, a 'surface tickle' may well be all that is required to achieve excellent weed kill. This means no more than 2 to 4 centimetres in depth.

Surface cultivation (not deep cultivation) can be repeated often to maintain a 'dry soil mulch' to retain soil moisture and kill young weeds. This technique is acceptable if done shallowly, usually 1 to 4 centimetres and is a good method if maintained for only 4 to 6 weeks while plants are young. Remember: for reasons explained elsewhere in this book, mulch or semi-permanent cover crops are preferred. Regular cultivation such as this is generally done with a hoe.

It's rarely necessary to dig deep unless you're developing a new garden bed for the first time, or digging out the underground parts of serious weeds. Deep digging, including double digging, is a useful strategy when establishing an annual garden on new ground. Double digging is a system for turning over subsoil as well as surface layers and incorporating organic matter throughout the soil profile. A trench is dug to one spade depth and the soil is removed to the side for replacement at the end of the job. A spit of subsoil (a layer that is equal depth to the length of the blade of a spade) is then turned over and organic matter added and mixed through. The trench is gradually advanced over the area to be developed and the soil from the first excavation is placed in the last trench.

Cultivation that takes place late in the season of annual crops will very likely damage surface roots and stop or retard the growth and maturity of crop or garden plants.

Soil disturbance brings new weed seeds to the surface. This causes them to germinate and therefore a series of shallow cultivations is always better than one deep cultivation. By revisiting the area frequently, we can ensure that the weed seedlings are small and therefore susceptible to cultivation. Constant or frequent tickling of the soil surface will eventually exhaust the supply of seed, but bare soil is also likely to be colonised by weeds coming in from wind or animals.

> Plant garlic and onions in blocks of four rather than in rows to facilitate cultivation around them. This permits the same number of plants to be grown per square metre, but provides more space around the plants for hoeing. Use care when cultivating in the vicinity of young seedlings or any small plants, as well as near established shallow-rooted plants such as citrus.

There is a wide range of different mechanical tools for cultivation in commercial organic agriculture. The emphasis is on shallow-working and deep-loosening, alternating the depth of working and stirring rather than chopping actions. For instance, there are power tools that stir the soil horizontally rather than chopping it like a rotary hoe. The stirring action collects underground roots and stolons and drags them to the soil surface where they dry out.

Stale seedbed

Stale seedbed (sometimes called a false seedbed) is a bed that is prepared for planting with a fine tilth. Instead of planting out, it is then left to go 'stale' — that is, it is left until weeds begin to grow.

It is then hoed very lightly to remove germinated weeds, but this is done with minimum disturbance so that few new seeds are brought to the surface to germinate in a second crop. Very light weeding may be repeated several times to remove most of the weed seeds near the soil surface before the main crop is planted.

I have seen very expensive and highly adjustable commercial machines designed to prepare and manage stale seedbed operations in small-scale commercial production. They neatly and gently slice off the surface of a prepared raised bed. I have also seen homemade versions of these machines. It is also possible to use a flame weeder on small weeds in a stale bed. The smaller the weeds, the less time and gas required — and this technique causes no soil disturbance.

The seedbed should be left at least 10 to 14 days in the tropics and an extra week in southern Australia.

EQUIPMENT
Hand tools
Some hand tools are specifically adapted to particular jobs. A basic set of weeding tools includes a trowel, bulb digger, garden fork, chop hoe and mattock, but there are endless versions of each. These tools can be adapted to a wide range of activities, but selecting the right tool and learning to use it well can save considerable time and labour. Some specialist tools, such as the stirrup hoe and a two-tined fork called a twork, are described below.

Selecting the right tool can be a very personal thing. I use a mattock where others would use a spade, fork or a hoe. Many gardeners have their favourite tool — that is part of the diversity of gardening. A favourite tool might be an old screwdriver for getting weeds out from between the pavers. It doesn't have to be an expensive creation to get the job done.

Hand trowel This useful tool is adaptable to many situations such as digging bulbs, getting under grass roots and for slicing

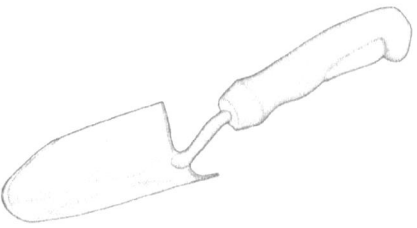

Drop-shank trowel

under small annual weeds. Choose one with a strong neck, possibly made from stainless steel. Narrow trowels are better for bulbs and transplanting. Trowels are personal tools. Shop around until you find one of strong construction that fits your hand well. The best design is called a drop-shank trowel, in which the handle is not in exactly the same plane as the mouth. The drop-shank shape is easier on the wrist.

Hand fork This is good for loosening soil, disturbing small seedlings and digging up fibrous roots. It's not as useful as a trowel for bulbs, however. Select one with round steel tines — it will be stronger than a flat blade.

Taproot digger This tool is specialised for digging bulbs. It is basically a strong shaft with a broader arrow head or short forked

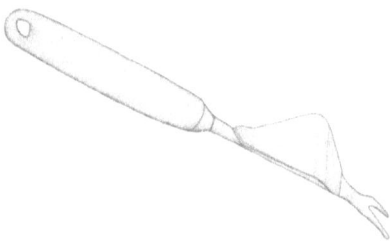

Taproot digger

end. It's designed for plunging into the soil and levering bulbs out. It is essential for digging an extensive area of really annoying weeds such as Oxalis. A typical taproot digger is 25 centimetres long with slight bend in the blade to provide a fulcrum. This tool has many names, including **bulb digger** and **daisy digger**.

Dock digger This old-fashioned tool is specialised for dock plants but will work on any large taproots. There are many different versions of dock diggers and a variety of homemade tools that do this job well.

Spade The spade is used for primary (initial) cultivation and digging holes. Because it may have a sharp blade it can also be used as a scraping tool to clear away surface growth. A spade can be used to loosen soil containing underground parts of weeds but a garden fork is generally preferred as it is less likely to cut up the underground parts of weeds that need to be thoroughly pulled from the soil.

Shovel A shovel is mainly for digging (pointed variety) or moving loose materials (square mouth). The square mouth version makes a reasonable scalping tool to cut through roots and skim off surface growth. It is easy to use a shovel in this way if soil is soft.

Garden fork This versatile tool is great for loosening soil containing weed roots, rhizomes or bulbs. It's less likely to sever underground parts, allowing runners to be pulled from the soil. Loosen the ground under bulbs and runners with a fork before extracting them. Remember that there are two common sizes of garden fork and different brands may vary considerably in width, length of tines and weight. Use the size that is best suited to your stature and to the job.

Twork This is a homemade two-tined fork invented by my mate and weed expert, David Duncan. Dave knows a great deal about weeding and originally invented this tool for watsonia removal, but it's good for bulbs and taproots as well. Find a good strong garden fork and cut off the outside two tines, leaving the complete footplate in place. It goes straight down under a watsonia corm and the two tines are very accurate, snagging roots less often. The twork is well suited to serious watsonia digging but a tool with similar properties is the NRG (pronounced *energy*) Pro Weeder. It looks much like a spade with an ergonomic round handle and a strong, reinforced stainless-steel blade that starts broad but becomes quite narrow. It is excellent for removing bulbs and corms and any deep roots.

Spin tiller This tool has a series of small 'ground driven' tines on a spindle that rolls freely. They are worked back and forth across the soil to 'tickle' the surface and are excellent for small weed seedlings. A spin tiller must have a suitably long handle to be efficient.

Mattock A mattock is one of my favourite weeding tools and versatile for heavier digging jobs. Use it to get underneath the large crown root of an old blackberry or to excavate below watsonia corms. It is possible to find light-weight and short-handled mattocks also. Find one that you can manage.

The U Bar This is a large and sturdy soil-aerating tool. It is used more for bed preparation than strictly for weed control, but sometimes these jobs go together. It can loosen soils to great depth and can do so without significant soil turning. The strong tines are pushed deep into the soil and the two tall handles that form the uprights of the U shape are pulled back, dragging the tines up and through the soil. This helps create slots that allow air and water movement deep into the soil without causing much inversion. Used a few times in the same spot, a U Bar can really help to deepen soil and break up hardpan. The handles are long to provide leverage, but this tool is not suited to tight clay soils. An Australian development is the **Gundaroo tiller**, a smaller but sturdy tool based on the same principles as the U Bar but much more applicable to home-garden use for serious row-crop gardeners.

Rake A rake can be pushed back and forth in soft, loose soil, effectively operating as a weeding tool, but in my opinion rakes are much more useful in collecting and removing material from the worksite. For instance, my favourite way to attack blackberry involves long- and short-handled secateurs, a brush hook, a rake, gloves, overalls, goggles and hat and a ladder. I drop the ladder into the bush, walk over the ladder with my protective gear, cut the fruiting canes and toss them out to family members who strip off the fruit, and remove other cut canes with the rake. A **rake-hoe** is the tool of choice for fire fighting and is a very fine tool for moving large amounts of soil and hoeing or scraping away weeds. It has a double-head with a broad hoe on one side and strong rake teeth on the other.

Hoe There's a huge variety of hoes. Some are designed for specific tasks and some have more versatility. Most cultures have a version of a hoe and they can be found in archaeological sites dating back 5,000 years.

Gardeners often have a favourite hoe that is suited to their physical ability, soil type and weed population. Some of my favourite hoes are not easy to find in commercial outlets. They may be antiques purchased at clearing sales and secondhand shops, old tools purchased at craft markets, local creations sold by blacksmiths or backyarders or available only online or from specialist importers. Some are homemade or are adaptations of other tools.

Finding the right tool is just the beginning; using the tool effectively and ergonomically is the next requirement. Sadly, many hoes come supplied with handles that are not strong enough for their purpose, and are too short or long for the user's height. A short handle requires the user to stoop forwards. A back bent forwards is much more subject to tiring and injury. I often find I have to replace the handles on garden tools with a longer and stouter version. Some of my tools come from specialist suppliers that provide a variety of working tools that can be easily attached to or detached from a handle. They make a very short handle for hands and knees work, a short handle for shorter people and a long handle for taller users. This allows me to have several different tools that can be moved between the very short and long handles. Some well-known brands provide this option.

Heavy draw (or 'chop') hoes can be used under a range of different soil conditions and will handle much drier soils than some of the hoes described here. The specialist hoes can be very sharp, accurate, fast and light, but they are best suited to small weeds and moist soil.

Understanding the weed target is also important. Hoeing may not be effective for very long if perennial weeds regrow from underground parts. Annual weeds are much more readily controlled by hoeing. Regular hoeing will rapidly erode the seed bank within a garden bed, so the interval between hoeing can be extended. The hoe should be used shallowly, however, so that deep weed seed is not brought up and so that plant roots and soil biology is not unduly disturbed. The dry soil mulch produced by regular shallow hoeing need only be 2 centimetres deep to be effective for controlling annual weed seedlings.

Hoeing must be done at flowering or before any seed can set. Roots must be severed completely at or below the soil surface and hoed weeds carted off to the compost heap or left on the soil surface to dry out and become mulch. Weeds immediately re-incorporated into the soil may grow again.

Hoes are seriously underestimated as a weed control tool. They are the tool of choice for many weeds in the home garden, but they are also ideal for controlling scattered weeds in crops and pasture. A little time spent with the hoe when weeds first appear would significantly reduce the need for herbicides to control weeds that have become well established. A very persistent person can control equally persistent weeds with a hoe.

Draw hoes are the most common hoe and utilise a downward chopping action. If sharp they may be simply drawn over the

Draw hoe

surface to cut small weeds. They have long been part of a basic gardening kit because of their versatility and because if a suitably heavy tool is purchased it can be used on very large weeds.

Push hoes have the sharp surface facing forward and are pushed through the soil just under the surface. They are good for small weeds. Select one with a long handle so you don't need to stoop forwards.

Dutch hoes have the sharp edge pointing forwards and slide along just under the soil surface. They are a very effective tool. My preferred version has a long sturdy handle and a pistol grip. These rugged and hardworking tools are so well engineered (with much attention to the correct angle of attachment of the blade and the handle) that they just glide over the soil, rather than digging into it.

Onion hoes have a semicircle of steel with the flat edge used to scrape or chop and the sharp corners used to pull out roots.

Stirrup hoes are a significant innovation. With a chip hoe, the down stroke is the work stroke and the up stroke only relocates the tool for the next work stroke. With a push hoe, the forward stroke is the work stroke and the back stroke simply relocates the tool. The stirrup hoe is sharp front and back, so that it can be drawn back and forth across the soil surface, with each stroke doing work. The stirrup is free to flip back and forth when pushed backwards or forwards, so that the sharp face is at the right angle of attack to dig into soil rather than slide over. For this reason it is sometimes called an **oscillating hoe**. When pulled back the stirrup flips so that the rear working face is at the right angle. The stirrup has rounded corners and the bottom surface is often slightly curved rather than flat so that the tool can be worked up close to garden or crop plants. With a bit of experience, a stirrup hoe is an effective tool for dealing with small weeds. It comes in a variety of sizes and the larger ones handle larger weeds, although it is not an ideal tool for very large weeds.

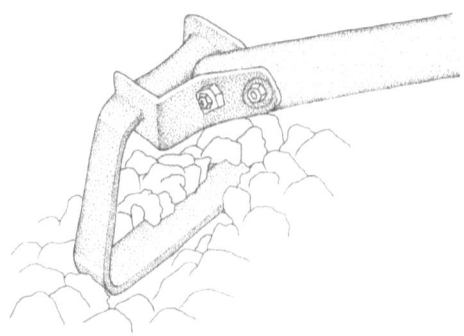

Stirrup hoe

Scuffle hoes are an innovation on the stirrup hoe. A scuffle hoe works back and forth but may not have the swivel action that keeps the sharp edge aligned at the right angle to the soil. Instead, it may have a design that works both ways without adjustment. It is unlikely to be as sharp (and therefore as effective) as the stirrup hoe.

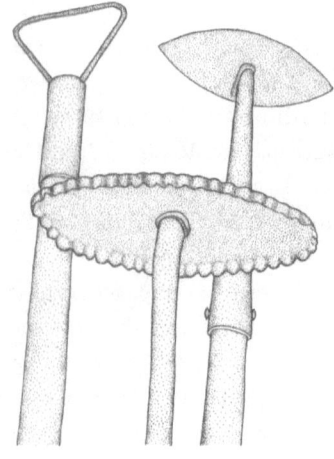

Scuffle hoes

Warren hoes are designed for cultivating between plants and for making furrows. The double-ended working part has a sharp edge for hoeing and two 'rabbit ear' points for furrowing.

Three-prong hoes are a common part of a garden toolkit (there are five-prong versions also). They are good for small annual weeds and if used carefully can also be useful for pulling runners from the soil. Soil needs to be moist and loose to be most effective for runners, but for annual weeds a prong hoe can be used to maintain a dry soil mulch. Some prong hoes are designed so that the prongs can be removed, which means you can replace a broken prong or convert the tool to a one-prong version for working in small spaces.

Wheel hoes are excellent for larger garden plots and small-scale vegetable or flower growers. They basically consist of a wheel, a toolbar and a handle. Many different working tools and soil management tools can be attached to the toolbar. Modern wheel hoes can have a light aluminium construction but are still sturdy — and with the right hoe attachments, versatile and fast.

Spin-tillers or **star hoes** have star-shaped wheels that turn in either direction. They work best on loose soil.

A **Ho-Mi** is a Korean tool with a curved blade that provides a convex and concave surface and a point. It is ideal for working with raised beds. It can be used to scoop, scrape and dig.

Coleman hoes, or 'gung hoes', are very effective tools for small weeds in favourable soils. They have a long handle and a sharp stainless-steel blade. As with most specialised hoes, a lot of thought and experience has gone into the angle of the 'goose-neck' that connects the blade and the handle, so that the hoe presents to the soil at exactly the right angle of attack. Eliot Coleman, an expert organic row-crop producer, invented the Coleman hoe. It adopts a completely different stance to the chip hoe and used correctly is much easier on your back. With a chip hoe, the handle is gripped with thumbs pointing down and this encourages the user to lean forwards, potentially destabilising them and harming the spine and back muscles. When using the Coleman hoe, stand erect with the hoe in front of your body and thumbs pointing up. The hoe is worked back and forth from left to right or towards and away from the body. As the blade is very sharp, experienced users also learn to position the hoe adjacent to the row of plants and simply walk forwards slicing through the soil. With use comes accuracy and this tool, when used well, is one of the fastest hoes you could find.

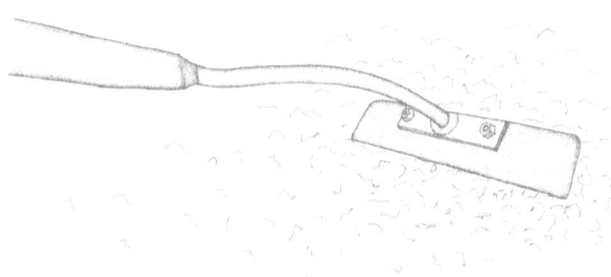

Coleman hoe

However, the sharp blade is not designed to deal with rocky soil and the lightweight construction means it is best for smaller weeds.

Canterbury forks have a hoe handle and a strong, three-prong fork-like tool. A well-made Canterbury fork is a very strong tool and can be used on larger established weeds.

Tim's top eight rules of hoeing

1. Maintain a sharp blade.
2. Completely sever weeds.
3. Depending on the weed species, it may be necessary to chop at or below the soil surface. Even weeds that will not normally regrow from underground parts may shoot from the main crown root just below the soil surface. A great deal of energy can be expended unnecessarily. It's best to chop weeds 'just deep enough' to segregate the growing parts from the roots.
4. Hoe when the surface soil is dry to encourage desiccation of plant roots. Disturb the surface just enough to create a dry mulch.
5. Hoe often. Smaller weeds require less effort to hoe, are quicker to dry out and easier to kill.
6. Use appropriate planting patterns so there is enough room between plants for a hoe.
7. Hoeing is rarely useful for perennial weeds.
8. Broadcast sowing makes better use of space if the soil is relatively weed free, but the result is that it's difficult to hoe. Rows are easier. Use grid planting (e.g. cluster planting of onions) for any crop with a high hoeing requirement, such as carrot or beetroot.

Shredders

Electric or petrol shredders are very useful tools for dealing with weeds that have been pruned or pulled. They are capable of reducing herbaceous or woody material into material suitable for composting or mulching.

Always investigate material to be mulched carefully to establish if there are seeds, small bulbs, cormils (small corms, usually produced on aerial stems) or nodes present that may survive the process. Compost suspect material before using on the garden.

Use hearing and eye protection, gloves and solid footwear when using petrol shredders.

Rotary hoes and digging machines

Rotary hoes, or rotovators, are petrol- or diesel-powered machines that chop the soil. Rotovating is a rapid way of turning a large area, but inevitably damages soil structure. It's generally unsuitable for controlling weeds that arise from stolons or rhizomes because it will chop and spread them through the soil, with each chopped part bearing a node capable of growing into a new plant. Even with non-stoloniferous weeds, it is generally necessary to rotovate several times in order to kill regrowth. It is best to add new organic matter such as compost to the soil when rotovating as this will help to repair structural damage from the disturbance to the soil profile.

A spading machine is less common but is much kinder to soil structure. Rather than thrashing the soil as the rotovator does, it has spade-shaped tines that delve into the soil and lift large clods, imitating the action of hand digging.

Mowing and slashing

Mowing at the correct height and at the right time can kill weeds, especially erect-growing broadleaf weeds. More often, mowing is simply a form of containment, where seed production is prevented

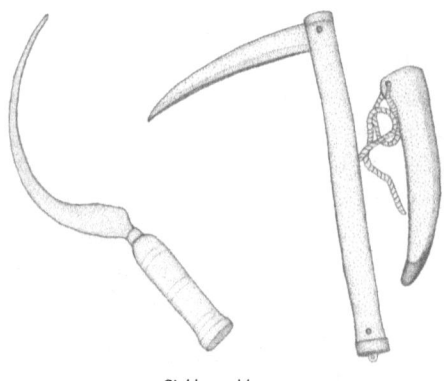

Sickle and kama

or limited and the overall vigour of the plant and quantity of photosynthetic material is reduced.

Hand mowing

Hand mowing with a sickle or scythe is useful to remove seeds from grasses and other weeds. Brush hooks, in many different shapes and sizes, are effective tools for cutting down blackberries or getting access to the trunk of weeds such as gorse so that they can be hand cut. In northern Australia, a machete is an essential tool for clearing weeds. A lightweight Asian-style sickle called a kama is also useful.

Power mowing

Mowing on a very low setting will knock off some invasive plants completely — gazanias being one example — however, the mowing must be severe and repeated. For many other plants, especially grasses and biennials, mowing can remove the seed stalk. Although the plant may replace the mowed stalk, it will not be as large and capable of supporting as many seeds as the original seed head. Some weeds have the ability to change shape (morphological plasticity). Plasticity refers to an ability to adopt different basic shapes depending on environmental pressures. Salvation Jane prefers to develop tall flower stalks, but if mown it will happily produce a shorter stalk and will do this repeatedly. If mown many times, a population of salvation Jane will form that is content to produce a shorter flower stalk and this will gradually take over. Regular mowing is still effective at reducing total seed numbers, but adaptability of the weed ensures that some survive.

Mowing will not generally kill weeds that are well adapted to living in the lawn because they establish a low coverage that escapes the mower blade. It may suppress seed production, however, and keep the lawn looking neat.

Brush-cutters

Brush-cutters and whipper snippers have the same limitations as mowers but are versatile tools, nonetheless. They are unlikely to actually eradicate weeds and, like mowers, there is always the danger that they spread weed seeds also. Try to use brush-cutters before weeds set seed.

Slashers and mowers

Slashers are hardworking and robust tools that are larger than an average domestic mower. For homeowners with a little more land to look after, the Heavy Cut mower is an excellent choice. Heavy Cut is an old design that has been made by various manufacturers over the past four decades or so.

It's a good, sturdy machine with very high wheels, giving it a significant advantage over other machines when used on uneven ground and in tight spaces. The wheels of smaller machines can become stuck in small depressions and dips. The Heavy Cut mower wheels ride through trenches and troughs, as well as up and over fallen logs. Some models have a wide (600-centimetre) wheelbase and a large, reliable engine.

The manoeuvrability of these walk-behind machines is excellent. If you apply the turning brake tightly, it is possible to turn while one wheel stays in place on the ground, just swivelling the machine around on the spot. The cutting blade is right out the front, with no jacking wheel to get in the way. This is the difference between a turf-type mowing machine, suitable only for lawns, and a really useful slasher for small properties, especially hilly ones. The front end can be lifted easily, by pushing down on the handles, which is useful when mowing grassy banks or for walking straight into large blackberry bushes or other weedy barriers.

Case study: mean machines

My Heavy Cut mower has an eight horsepower motor, four forward gears and reverse. I thought this was a monster, until I saw my mate Brian's machine.

Brian Billing modified his Heavy Cut mower (the Hillside model) by extending both the blades and the wheelbase to include a 32-inch (80-centimetre) cutter and motorbike tyres. He also swapped to a 12 horsepower engine. The larger engine and knobbly tyres provide excellent cutting ability on steep slopes, with plenty of traction for going up or across the slope.

For 14 years I managed about 20 hectares of steep country with a slasher, a petrol brush-cutter and hand tools.

A significant advantage in the young orchard was to raise the irrigation up above the ground.

I slung the lines from short wooden stakes while the new orchard trees were young. As the trees grew, the lines were transferred to hanging from an appropriate forked branch in the tree itself, with occasional stakes where needed. The front blades of the mower could be poked under the line, which was about at knee height. I became very skilled and

> fast at this job. I recommend to everyone starting a new plantation that they consider raising the irrigation. The disadvantage is that you cannot cross-mow; however, my slopes at Basket Range were too steep for cross-mowing anyway. Another advantage is that when the line is turned on, you can see every dripper or sprinkler working, and don't need to bend and lift to check each emitter.
>
> Michael Plane and Joyce Wilkie also use a Heavy Cut mower on their farm at Gundaroo. They are clever users and designers of hand tools, and have installed an excellent addition to their machine. It is a small bar that projects forward just above the blade. It enables them to cut long grass cleanly, which might otherwise wrap around the blade and jam it up. The bar pushes the grass over, so the blade swings around and cuts it just at the point of most tension, slicing cleanly through rather than tugging at the stems.

Mowing techniques

By setting the mowing height very low and using repeated passes mowing can be aimed at eradicating weeds, but is more often just a holding technique. It is aimed at reducing seed set and reducing the quantity of biomass held in the weeds. Nutrients contained in the biomass can then be recycled and sent back into the soil, and into crop or garden plants. It may be necessary to permit some flowering if you want the groundcover to survive. If you want to provide shelter and nectar or pollen for beneficial insects, you also need to allow flowering. Most commercial organic orchardists use cover crops under their trees, mowing them to feed the soil but also retaining some for habitat. They won't mow the entire property at once, perhaps mowing only every second row, and following up several weeks later by mowing the alternate rows.

In the tropics, weeds such as Singapore daisy (*Sphagneticola trilobata*) survive mowing very well and make an excellent cover crop. Try to avoid spreading seed of species such as wandering Jew (*Tradescantia albiflora*).

Leaving some weeds long enough provides a source of nectar, pollen and habitat, as well as protecting the soil. But there are also other good reasons to permit weeds to grow tall. As plants grow up, so their roots grow down. As roots grow down and through the soil, they leave behind organic matter that is slewed off as the root tip pushes through the soil. Roots also exude polysaccharides into the soil. Polysaccharides are long-chain sugars. They are sometimes thought of as waste products, but are much more than that. These gum-like substances glue soil together, creating habitat and food for microorganisms.

Up to 30 per cent of the products of photosynthesis are exuded into the soil. In doing so, the plant creates ideal conditions for its own growth and for the soil organisms that recycle organic matter and make available nutrients. Soil organisms also manufacture chemical products that fight disease. Penicillium bacteria, for example, are natural soil-dwelling organisms. The penicillin they release into the soil may be taken up by plants and used to help them to control plant pathogens.

The area around the roots of plants, called the rhizosphere, is the most biologically active and diverse part of the soil. It is here that plant food is produced by organisms, just where plants need it. Plants also control the rate at which these nutrients are transformed and made available. Sun and temperature drive photosynthesis and movement of sap up and down within the plant. This in turn determines the rate of exudation and that affects the level of biological activity in the rhizosphere.

The concept of the rhizosphere is critical to the idea of organic growing and how to drive it. Indeed, while it is a popular conception that surface additions of organic matter builds the organic soil profile, experienced organic growers will tell you that only plant roots can build a really organic soil. The rhizosphere is the powerhouse of activity — it's where nutrients, enzymes, vitamins and other health-giving properties are transformed and transferred. Learning to grow plant roots is indeed the key to building organic soil.

Plant roots push down through the soil, opening it up, breaking through hardpans and bringing nutrients from deep down back up through the soil profile. When the tops of plants are grazed or mown off, the capacity of the plant to produce photosynthetic products is reduced and consequently the quantity of roots that can be supported is reduced. Some roots therefore die, and this opens up spaces within the soil and encourages aerobic organisms to break down the discarded roots, adding organic matter at depth. This process can greatly increase soil depth and volume over time, and is sometimes called 'the carbon gift'.

Crimped rollers

Some commercial organic producers use a technique called a crimped roller to roll down aggressive grasses such as paspalum (family Poaceae) and Johnson grass (*Sorghum halepense*). If grasses are driven over or trampled they will very likely just pop up again. The addition of a few crimps on the roller cracks or breaks the stems, and they are unlikely to recover. If done at the right time in summer crimping can be very effective. This method does not kill the grass, which will continue to provide soil protection and the grass will return in the following season.

This is an another excellent example of how a different way of looking led to a cheap and manageable organic solution for a weed problem, while inability to move outside traditional concepts of what is a weed befuddled the non-organic neighbours. The neighbours looked in and saw only an intractable weed for them, one they feared and attempted (unsuccessfully) to eliminate using herbicides. They were distrustful of organic growers incorporating weeds into their management plan. From the organic growers' perspective, they had a vigorous smothering cover crop that they could manage by regular mowing and a single timely pass with a crimped roller, costing almost nothing (made from scrap steel on the farm), while recycling the organic matter and building soil carbon and fertility.

Carting away weeds

Pulled, dug or hoed weeds may be left on the soil surface as mulch if they do not contain seeds, nodes or underground parts capable of growing. Weeds with growing parts may be thoroughly dried out on a garden path or other hard surface and then mulched or composted. Composting is the best option because the heat of the compost destroys any remaining viable buds or seeds.

Here are some useful tools for carting away weeds:

- **Garden barrows** These come in many shapes and sizes. Use one that is appropriate to your size and strength.
- **Garden bags** These large, tough canvas or poly bags can carry as much as a barrow, but without the convenience of wheels. They are good for getting up close to a job and are easy to tip into a compost bin.
- **Canvas or poly tarpaulins** Spread the canvas or tarp out, load it up with clippings or pulled weeds and drag it away. They can hold a great deal of material. Even if weeds are later transferred to another vessel, using a sheet of tough material stops weeds tossed down from shedding seeds or bulbils that might grow later onto the soil.
- **Cardboard boxes** Large boxes make excellent weed receptacles. I collect them from my local electrical goods manufacturer. They can be used to increase the capacity of a garden barrow, they are easily loaded onto a sack truck (hand trolley) and they keep weed propagules isolated from the soil.

TURN UP THE HEAT — THERMAL CONTROL
Naked flame

Flame has always been an important part of weed control, for clearing brush and disposing of seed and other propagules. Grandpa may well have used a kerosene burner to control weeds under the barbed wire fence. Burning will always be important, although we know that composting, chipping and mulching are generally better for the atmosphere and the carbon cycle. I do use fire to remove old stumps and occasionally for fuel removal in a fire-control boundary prior to summer. When I first removed a large patch of broom from the garden, I used a moving sequence of very small fires to 'smoke' the seed, thereby causing '10 years' seed' to germinate in two seasons (see page 188).

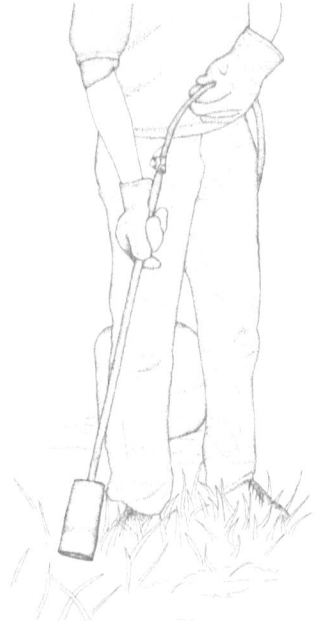

A hand-held burner

Naked flame has some limitations, chiefly that it cannot be safely used in some weather conditions, especially on fire ban days, or over flammable mulch. However, flame provided by a simple gas burner, available from your local gasfitter, is an effective and easy-to-use tool for controlling weeds in the home garden. It completely comes into its own as a replacement for herbicides in the control of weeds in gravel driveways and paths.

It is not necessary or desirable to 'burn' the target weed — indeed, this would destroy the organic matter, which we would prefer to keep for recycling and soil improvement. High temperature applied for a relatively short time is sufficient to kill the plant. Heat causes the water inside plant cells to expand, rupturing the cell wall and spilling the contents. After the flaming, the weed may just look a little yellow, but should die over the next few days. It may be necessary to hover the flame over the centre of strong rosettes (for example young salvation Jane) or grasses (because their growing tip is preserved low down on the plant), but the time spent per weed should be minimised to reduce energy use. About 90 to 100ºC for one-tenth of a second is enough heat to control smaller seedlings, with ideal results from temperatures of 130 to 140ºC.

Weeds are most susceptible to thermal control when they are young because they lack thick outer surfaces or the internal reserves to regrow from heat damage. Once weeds reach about 5 centimetres tall or get past the three- to five-leaf stage, they will require more energy to kill. Smaller than this and less than one second of direct heat will kill them.

In order to test that sufficient heating has occurred to kill the target, use the fingerprint test. Simply press the treated but still green leaf between finger and thumb. A lasting fingerprint should remain.

In commercial operations, a 'pre-sprouting window', or germination test row, is used to flame the soil free of weeds just before a seed crop emerges. In this technique, which is useful in crops that are very susceptible to early-stage weeds (such as carrot) a double row of seed is planted two to three days prior to the main crop. When the early rows emerge, you know that the main crop is about to emerge, and can flame the soil to kill any weeds that are already present and would have a slight edge on the young crop. An alternative method is to leave a small portable greenhouse, or even

Tim's five essential tips for flame weeders

1. It takes some practice to learn how to use a flame weeder well. Once the technique is mastered, the speed of weeding can be much increased and the quantity of gas used reduced.
2. It's not necessary or desirable to burn the weed, only to dry it out to the extent that the growing point dies. This can often be achieved with high heat, but for only a short time.
3. In strong daylight, remember half of the gas flame will be invisible to you. It is easy to think you are holding the tool well above the target weed, but in fact the flame is being dissipated rather than concentrated. The bit you cannot see is the blue flame, which is actually hotter than the visible yellow flame.
4. Start the flame weeder at dusk when daylight is rapidly fading. You will be able to see the entire flame. Try to fix an image of how long the flame really is and use the visual image of the flame to fix the correct height in your mind. Depending on the design of the burner you may find the invisible part is twice the length of the visible flame.
5. Any thermal weed control method works better on dry soils and weeds.

an old window, lying on the ground. The warming effect of the window/greenhouse will cause the seed underneath to germinate slightly early, and indicates when the flaming technique should be applied to the remainder of the bed.

Because the growing tip of monocotyledons is protected at the base of the stem, they are a little more resistant to heat treatment than broadleaf weeds. The system can still be used, however, with some selectivity, such as in onions or leeks.

Steam

Steam is also used to sterilise soil (both potting soils and in situ soils) but is not an activity that should be undertaken by home gardeners. It requires the operation of a commercial steam boiler and a trained boilermaker attendant. Large quantities of fuel and water are required in this method and it is not a cheap option.

Steam, often with the addition of foaming additives, is also used to burn weeds and several commercial machines are available. Local governments sometimes use steam for weed control in public places with much passing foot traffic, such as inner-city streets, parks, bus stops, playgrounds, and in environmentally sensitive areas such as adjacent to waterways. Thermal weed controls are ideal for this use because pesticides are not easy to use safely in close proximity to human activity and can harm aquatic animals.

Hot water

Steam requires a bit of skill, but hot water is easy to come by. Small areas of weeds can be treated effectively with a kettle of hot water. This technique is particularly useful for killing small weeds emerging between pavers close to the house.

Controlled burning

Selective burning with small bonfires or controlled burns is a useful method to remove clumps of impenetrable weeds such as blackberry, lantana and gorse, and to destroy rubbish remaining after removing pernicious weeds such as watsonia or Cape tulip (*Homeria* species). Burning, or more correctly the 'smoking' resulting from burning, may also break the dormancy of some seeds such as gorse (*Ulex europaeus*), English broom (many subspecies in five genera) and apple of Sodom (*Solanum hermanni*), which makes them accessible to control.

Always check fire restrictions with your local council and take necessary precautions to prevent fire spreading or personal injury. Burning may also activate the soil seed bank to cause more weed invasion, so the burnt area will require follow-up.

Burning should be an occasional activity only to solve serious access problems and remove persistent propagules, such as watsonia corms. Regular burning destroys organic matter that should be returned to the soil.

Soil solarisation

Solarisation is a thermal technique that uses heat from the sun. It can be used to kill weed seeds at or near the soil surface and to kill soil-borne plant diseases and nematodes. The method uses clear plastic and should be undertaken in summer or in seasons when there is significant exposure to solar radiation, including clear skies combined with high temperatures.

To solarise soil, follow these simple steps:
- prepare the bed for planting, including the removal of surface vegetation (weed and crop residues) and levelling
- if the soil is not at field capacity, irrigate to that point
- cover the area with clear plastic. Toss soil over the edges of the plastic to seal air in and hold the sheets down
- the plastic should remain in place long enough to heat soil to a depth of 15 centimetres. This will generally take at least four weeks in tropical areas and in southern Australia during midsummer

- repair any rips that develop immediately using strong tape or soil to hold the plastic down
- remove the plastic and plant out immediately to maximise the ensuing weed free period.

The plastic must sit close to the soil surface. Growing weeds remaining underneath the plastic will severely impair the heating of the soil and the plastic may become a 'greenhouse', increasing the growth rate of the weed. Soil must be practically bare before the plastic is laid.

The black plastic technique

Some weeds and grasses that grow from stolons or rhizomes are very difficult to control, for example kikuyu (*Pennisetum clandestinum*), buffalo (*Stenotaphrum secundatum*) and couch (*Cynodon dactylon*). The black plastic technique can be very useful for these difficult weeds and is completely effective in some situations. Used in combination with other techniques, such as pH or fertility modification, and digging and mulching, the black plastic technique is probably the best option for good control of stoloniferous plants without herbicides. The system works best in hot weather and may only be completely effective in summer or autumn in southern Australia.

I first discovered this technique intuitively when gardening around a house built on short poles. The kikuyu from one side of the yard had grown under the house and I started pulling at one piece. It had grown diagonally under the building, going right through to the other side. I pulled it up and wrapped it around my arm, much like rolling up a hose or a rope. At the other extreme there was a healthy 2.5 metres of vigorously growing kikuyu. I was amazed at the persistence of the kikuyu, which just kept growing through, searching for the light. This incident led to me developing the technique described here.

Botany basics — stolons and rhizomes

Buffalo and couch grow from stolons, and kikuyu grows from rhizomes and stolons. For simplicity, the term rhizome is used in this description of the black plastic technique, but the same techniques work for kikuyu, buffalo and couch.

A rhizome is a specially adapted root that stores starch for future growth and is well supplied with nodes (potential growing points). A stolon is an adaptation from a stem. It travels above the ground and the nodes give rise to roots and shoots. In an established patch, there can be lots of rhizome or stolon, and consequently lots of stored starch. This is one reason that just pulling or mowing will not be an effective control. The plant simply re-grows from reserves stored underground. Another reason is because many grasses that have this adaptation are also very effective at photosynthesis. As soon as the first green tips appear they rapidly produce starch and store it away in the underground parts. And as if this isn't enough, the rhizomes tend to break at the node points, so that many small parts are left under the surface, each with the potential to regrow.

Some rhizomes may go deep, but in most situations they are found in the top 150 millimetres of soil. Vertical fibrous roots go down from the rhizomes and in some cases rhizomes or roots may reach 4 metres depth (in the case of kikuyu), but deep roots are chiefly for obtaining water and produce little or no regrowth.

The rhizomes must be weakened or removed. Digging is effective on some soil types and when soil is at the

> correct moisture content. When these conditions apply, the rhizomes will readily give up their grip on soil and can be pulled away without leaving too many sections in the ground. In heavy clay soils or at low moisture levels hand-pulling will leave too many sections of rhizome in the ground for effective control.

Laying the plastic

Before laying the black plastic, adjust the mower to the lowest setting and mow all grass and weeds to the ground. Water the area well. The plant must be actively growing; any stresses that slow growth, such as low temperatures or dry soil will slow down the effectiveness of this technique.

Lay the plastic next. If possible, go right to the edge of the infestation. If you cannot lay plastic to the end, or to a natural edge such as a track or pathway, you will need to treat a large minimum area. This is because the rhizomes form a large mass of connected (and even self-grafted) roots and will transfer starch from exposed green tips back to the rhizomes. Alternatively, you can trench or slice deeply around the edge of the treated area, but you will have to maintain this barrier during treatment.

Hold the plastic down by trenching and throwing soil over the edge of the sheet. You can also use logs, bricks and other heavy objects. Leave the plastic on the ground as long as possible. Depending on the season (whether the grasses are growing vigorously), the amount of underground parts and the thickness of the plastic, this will probably be at least three to five weeks. Check under the plastic occasionally to monitor growth of the grass.

The plant will regrow under the plastic mulch. The rhizomes give rise to new shoots, which wander around under the plastic, trying to find the light. The new growth will be 'etiolated'. This term refers to long inter-nodal spaces (a long distance between nodes or swellings on the stem) and the bleached white colour. Most plants will do this when deprived of adequate light. There may be a touch of green because even black plastic will not prevent all sunlight from getting through. The new growth will be predominantly white or a pale yellow. The pale colour is due to lack of chlorophyll, the enzyme responsible for photosynthesis. It is usually green in land-based plants, but may also be red. Chlorophyll is only produced by the plant in response to exposure to sunlight (otherwise it would be a waste of energy). It also protects the plant from ultra-violet radiation (UV). This is why the black plastic technique works so well.

The plant has now expended much of the stored energy from the rhizomes in producing a great length of etiolated growth, which wanders around under the plastic looking for light. The next step is to wait for a very hot day — the hotter the better. Sometime around or just after midday, in the hottest part of the day, pull back the black plastic.

The tender, pale, etiolated growth will be severely sunburnt and will die. Leave it exposed for the whole day or for a second day and then mow it to the ground again. Do not mow too early — such is the tenacity of these plants that even these nodes in their stressed, etiolated growth may still be capable of developing. This technique is really a form of thermal or heat treatment; it's the hot rays of the sun that actually kill the etiolated parts.

Dig down and visually inspect the underground parts. Healthy rhizomes are white, turgid (firm) and full or solid to the feel. Severely stressed or expended rhizomes are not bright white and may appear flaky or empty when squeezed.

The technique on its own is unlikely to be completely effective the first time, but may be repeated, or the rhizomes may have been weakened to the point where hand-digging or thick mulching will be effective.

In very difficult situations, such as under shady trees or in winter (southern Australia) the technique may need to be repeated two or three times.

Troubleshooting the black plastic method
Are the weeds not dying? Having a few problems? This list may help:
- soil moisture must be adequate before the plastic is placed, otherwise the grasses will not be stimulated to grow
- manures or fertilisers may also be added prior to laying down plastic as they may stimulate growth
- the plastic must be held down tightly at the edges, preferably trenched in or covered with soil, to exclude as much light as possible
- punctures to the plastic may be repaired by laying another piece over the top. Do this quickly: once the grass starts to photosynthesise it can store food away rapidly
- check around the edge of the plastic to ensure that bits of rhizome or stolon are not growing out from under the plastic or up from the ground (they may transfer starch back to the covered rhizomes)
- this technique may work well with other weeds too, but is a very useful strategy for grasses with stolons or rhizomes.

In cool or cloudy conditions where the sun is not strong enough to damage etiolated growth, remove the plastic, mow away all the etiolated growth and replace the plastic. In this case the technique works by starch exhaustion only, rather than a combination of exhaustion and burning.

OTHER APPROACHES
Ozone
At the time of writing, ozone is not viable as a soil sterilisation method, but it's rapidly becoming the choice for sterilising

operations in organic food processing because it leaves no residue. Methods for killing weed seeds in the soil may evolve in the future.

Biological weed control

Research into biological weed control is an expensive and long-term operation, but once the biocontrol agent has been isolated, introductions and control are potentially cheap, provided that the biocontrol agent is self-maintaining. Expense and time are required both to find a natural enemy and then to ensure that there will be a high level of host specificity, so that non-target native, productive and ornamental plants will not be harmed.

Natural enemies

The natural enemies of weeds include diseases, nematodes and insects, and they can all be used as control agents. Australia has been a world leader in weed biocontrol since the famous use of the *Cactoblastis* moth to control prickly pear (*Opuntia* species). The larvae of the *Cactoblastis* eat the prickly pear leaves and seed pods, and its release in Australia virtually destroyed prickly pear populations. There are many recent examples of release of control agents, including rust for blackberry, the rust fungus *Puccinia chondrillina* for skeleton weed control, and weevils for *Salvinia* (an aquatic weed) and salvation Jane.

Mycoherbicides are substances derived from disease-causing (pathogenic) fungi. They may be a live fungus organism (usually spores) or an extract of the toxic component. Mycoherbicides are available for weeds such as velvetleaf (*Abutilon theophrasti*), prickly sida (*Sida spinosa*) and sicklepod (*Cassia obtusifolia*).

There are many hundreds of biological control research projects underway in Australian universities, departments of agriculture, and National Parks and Wildlife Services. Biocontrol agents will become much more common in the near future and many more weeds will succumb to natural enemies. Biological control has some major advantages — it's self-perpetuating, selective in attack, has no residues and has the ability to persist in the environment by using wind, water and other natural distribution mechanisms to seek out host weeds.

Grazing animals

Grazing animals are an important form of weed control and many landowners on small acreage use sheep, goats, poultry and sometimes other animals such as domestic rabbits and guinea pigs for this purpose. On larger acreage, horses, cattle, alpaca and other animals are also useful.

Poultry are the easiest grazing animals to control on small allotments, using a selection of methods including:
- free-range poultry, where space permits
- portable chicken houses
- permanent or temporary fences including electro-net (lightweight electrified mesh).

Chickens, bantams, geese, ducks, guineafowl and other breeds are all effective. Geese are often used on organic farms, usually under perennial vegetation. Chinese weeder geese have a more vegetarian diet and are smaller, so they trample garden vegetation less. Poultry need to be kept away from young vegetables and fruiting crops. They also require water, shade and protection from foxes, hawks and eagles. Portable electrified net fences are available for restraining poultry and keeping predators out.

Rabbits and **guinea pigs** in portable houses are also useful. One of the most remarkable examples of weed control with grazing animals I have seen was the case of organic vegetable grower Lex Langridge in Western Australia. Lex farmed carrots in an area that was susceptible to carrot nematode, so he needed to remove every bit of carrot root from the soil to ensure that a short rotation cycle was effective at stopping the reproductive cycle of the pest. After the carrot crop, Lex put up a short electric fence sufficient to pen several small pigs (not guinea pigs) that rooted out the remaining broken carrots. Then he removed the pigs and brought out a portable chicken house and some U-shaped mesh frames that fitted over the bed. The chickens got anything green that remained and any grubs left in the soil. The pigs and chicken replaced the need for primary cultivation, so Lex was able to replant after a light tickle. When the seedlings were well established, he placed a portable house between the beds with guinea pigs. The guinea pigs would destroy young leafy spinach, but once the spinach was more than 15 centimetres high, they were not really interested. Even smaller zucchini could be grazed, because they have little spiky projections all over the plant. So Lex knew what age each crop had to be before he could graze it. The guinea pigs loved the shelter of leafy crops because their main predators are birds of prey. Because the beds were far apart and the guinea pigs would not venture out into the open, they did not stray into the recently planted areas. Even better, if Lex did want them to visit another bed, he simply screwed together some plastic conduit. The guinea pigs soon learned that a change of diet was waiting at the end of the pipe and enthusiastically raced down in the expectation of a meal. Brilliant and cheap, and the zoo was ready to take any excess guinea pigs.

Goats are often staked on roadsides or steep land for weed control near where I live. Unfortunately, many of them lead a sorry life, with lots of blackberry, not enough variety, scant fresh water and almost no freedom to roam. I cannot keep permanently tethered animals, but I can sometimes put tethered sheep or goats on weedy areas. Intensive grazing by goats can seriously reduce otherwise difficult weeds such as variegated thistle (*Silybum marianum*), saffron thistle (*Carthamus lanatus*) and serrated tussock (*Nassella trichotoma*).

I have learned from organic orchardists that shorter breeds of **sheep** are excellent in orchards. Merinos are tall and have strong back legs, so they can stand like a goat and sometimes browse on the fruit trees. Suffolks, on the other hand, have short legs and they are less likely to stand on their hind legs at all.

Pigs are fabulous at rooting around in soil looking for edible rhizomes and will help to clean up weeds such as bracken. Slash the bracken tops and rake away or burn them before putting the pigs in so that you avoid poisoning them from the mature fronds.

Cross-grazing with more than one type of livestock is useful, because each will have grazing preferences and habits that can contribute to weed control. It will also reduce the likelihood of preferential grazing by a single species, giving rise to weeds that are not palatable by that species. Be aware that some weeds are poisonous in smaller or larger doses; some that can be lightly grazed will kill stock that are forced to consume too much. Ragwort (*Senecio jacobaea*) will damage cattle, and salvation Jane will harm horses, but sheep can cross-graze in both situations and can handle much more ragwort and salvation Jane in their diet. Cattle cross-grazed with sheep will control St John's wort (*Hypericum perforatum*).

Organic herbicides

Salt has been used as a herbicide for millennia. It is reasonably non-selective, however, and large quantities are required. Apart from salt, the idea of an organic herbicide was for many years anathema to some, yet a holy grail to others. Many farmers who were otherwise interested in conversion to organic practices could not bring themselves to abandon the ease of synthetic herbicides; on the other hand, some organic advocates reserved their most vitriolic criticism of chemical farming methods for herbicides. Synthetic herbicides were not available until 1946 but quickly grew to be 50 per cent of world pesticide sales. Much of our farming system was then designed around an annual cycle of herbicide use.

Petroleum oils, especially diesel and turpentine, have been used from time to time, but they have not passed the test of permissibility in certified organic production.

In the 21st century, organic herbicides have finally arrived and the first such products are available in Australia. Two types of products have been released — one being vinegar and the other an essential oil-based product.

Vinegar — simple acetic acid (but possibly stronger than ordinary table vinegar) — is a herbicide. It is made by diluting commercial-strength vinegar and it can be purchased from garden centres in a ready-to-use trigger pack. It works by dissolving the outer waxy cuticle of the leaf, causing it to rapidly dry out.

Corn gluten meal is used as a specialised herbicidal mulch in the USA. It works by leaching strong allelopathic chemicals into the soil and suppresses germination. Corn gluten meal is not readily available in Australia, although some **oilseed meals** and **fruit pulp** have a similar effect. **Fruit pomace** (residue from squeezing juice) also provides a natural source of acetic acid that kills young weeds.

More recently a range of plant-derived herbicides has emerged in organic farming, including a variety of products based on plant essential oils. In the USA, these herbicides are available with ingredients such as acetic acid and lemon oil, citrus and pelargonium oils on their own, and cinnamon and clove oils in combination. Research indicates that many essential oils, including tea tree and calendula have herbicidal, fungicidal and insecticidal properties.

In Australia and New Zealand, one organically approved herbicide product made from essential oils is commercially available. At the time of writing, another product based on pelargonic acid is also available in Australia but the active ingredient is synthetic and therefore it has not been approved by the certification bodies. Individual organic gardeners may decide this is good enough and choose to use the product, even though it is based on an imitation of natural pelargonic acid, whereas certified growers are restrained from access at present.

> ## Organic herbicides and certified organic farming
>
> Until recently there were no herbicides permitted in certified organic production. Some biological herbicides, sometimes called bio-rational herbicides, have been around for several decades, mainly based on fungal spores or extracts, but these products are rarely used on organic farms. They are generally treated by the certification bodies as biological controls, which are permitted by organic standards. An example of a bio-rational herbicide from Australia is the fungi *Colletotrichum orbiculare* used for control of Bathurst burr (*Xanthium spinosum*).

New generation of herbicide

A new generation of plant-derived herbicides has been approved for use in certified organic agriculture. They have both a knockdown and pre-emergent action, are non-systemic and not translocated within the plant. The first product on the market is sometimes known as pine oil, but it is not a simple pine oil product. The active ingredients and the synergist compounds are all specific extracts from the distillation of pine oil. Significant intellectual property attaches to the specific fractions of pine oil that are most effective for use as a herbicide.

Organic herbicides work by dissolving the lipid layer that protects soft plant tissues, stripping the outer coat off the leaves and seeds and therefore causing desiccation. They will not work against lignified material (the material from which roots and stems are made) and therefore can be used close against vine or tree stems and in high volumes to destroy seeds on or near the soil surface without causing harm to established plants

Organic herbicides only remain active in soil or on the plant for a very short time and can be used 24 hours prior to seeding cover crops without affecting germination. They do not have any significant affect on soil biology, birds, bees, microbes or plant roots. The withholding period from grazing stock is very short — stock may be returned to pasture when the plant is dry.

They are also an excellent tool for controlling herbicide resistance and reduce the weed seed bank over time with successive applications. Any overspray results only in localised damage because it is not translocated.

Organic herbicides are essentially non-selective in their mode of action but can be very selective by modifying the method of application. Broadleaf weeds, especially in the rosette stage of growth, provide a large surface area for easy coverage. Grasses require much higher volumes of tank mix because the growing point is located at the base of the plant and is often well protected by the leaf lamina (the flattened portion of the leaf). Levels of application must be adjusted to provide appropriate coverage.

Organic herbicides may also be used to stop seed development. I have a steep site where I do not want to remove plant cover and increase the risk of erosion. In this situation, lower rates of application are sufficient to kill developing seed and prevent the weed seed bank from increasing until more permanent measures are established. Seeds, like leaves, are covered in a waxy coating that is dissolved by essential oils. This causes the seed to desiccate and also become exposed to pathogens.

It is even possible to control very difficult weeds such as caltrop (*Tribulus terrestris*) but the best approach is to apply it early in the growth cycle before the seed case has hardened.

An economic case for the use of organic herbicide is at least partly determined by considering not just the cost on one application, but also a gradual decrease in the soil seed bank after repeated applications.

Organic herbicides are sometimes added to conventional herbicides, especially if the problem of herbicide activity on any particular target is penetration. It will help by dissolving waxy outer layers or fine leaf hairs that prevent absorption and therefore increases the efficiency of other herbicides. For example, periwinkle (*Vinca* spp.) is very difficult to kill with a conventional herbicide alone, but results improve with the addition of organic herbicides. Compatibility with every herbicide type cannot be guaranteed and it may be useful to refer to an organic herbicide manufacturer or your supplier's agronomist for case-study reports prior to use. In some states, off-label permits may also be required (off-label permits are issued when herbicides are used for purposes not included on the product label, when authorities agree that there is slim chance of negative effects). Organic herbicides can also be a useful tool for preventing herbicide resistance.

Critical application methods Organic herbicide must be applied using the correct nozzle and pump combinations to deliver increased volumes to the target. Application instructions vary from traditional herbicide practices because plant-derived herbicides are essentially a different product. Because they are derived from plants they have a much shorter active life and are not translocated, therefore requiring increased rates of coverage. Whereas runoff in most herbicide application situations is completely unacceptable, run off to the soil with the application of organic herbicide helps to kill off any weed seeds at the soil surface.

Plant extracts make effective herbicides

Early adopters of plant-derived herbicides in organic production report success with control of a range of broadleaf weeds, especially if application is made while the target is reasonably small. Plant-derived herbicides are a useful tool for organic and biodynamic producers, but to understand the economics of their use it is necessary to consider the pre-emergent effect over successive applications as well as the contact kill. Economically it is unlikely to compare favourably with conventional herbicides but most users will not expect the product to be a substitute for glyphosate. It does permit organic growers to clean weeds from around sprinkler heads, machinery parking areas, buildings and other infrastructure.

The first commercially released, patented, plant-derived herbicide in Australia is now on the market. Australian release of competing 'off the shelf' organic herbicides available in the northern hemisphere can be expected in the near future.

SPECIAL ENVIRONMENTS
Woody weeds
Established woody weeds require some different strategies to keep them in order. Smaller woody weeds can simply be grubbed or pulled, but as they grow they will establish root systems that are extensive and have a strong grip on the ground.

Cutting or felling
Cutting down larger woody weeds such as camphor laurel (*Cinnamomum camphora*) or cotoneaster is effective but you will need to control sucker growth. For example, radiata pine (*Pinus radiata*) or many weedy *Acacia* species cut right to the ground will not regrow from the stump. But they are likely to grow again if they are not cut right to the soil surface. The adventitious buds that give rise to new shoots are found up the stem just under the bark, but they stop just above the crown root. If the cut is made below the level of the buds it cannot reshoot. If roots very close to the ground level are scuffed they may also reshoot, but they will not grow if left intact, and therefore these weeds can be removed with a handsaw or chainsaw.

Ringbarking
Ringbarking will also work for weeds such as radiata pine but the same problem of adventitious buds recurs. The cut should be deep enough to stop all sap flow through the cambium layer and should be made low to the ground. Be aware also that a large woody weed will contain considerable resources within the above-ground

tissues and may take some time to die, perhaps long enough for seed held on the plant to mature, leading to reinfestation.

Removing with a tree-popper

The tree-popper is an excellent tool for removing woody shrubs and small trees such as broom and gorse. It has jaws that close around the bush, a curved roller plate that sits on the ground and a strong handle. The tool provides easy leverage when the handle is pushed down, and the shrub pops out of the ground. Use it on boneseed, *Acacia* species, boxthorn (*Lycium ferocissimum*), briar rose (*Rosa rubiginosa*) or any woody weeds. It's not as effective on woody weeds with brittle wood such as hawthorn (*Crataegus* species), which is inclined to snap when being pulled out.

Using mechanical tools

Much larger woody weeds or very large areas of infestation require removal with mechanical tools. There are excellent devices designed for this purpose, such as large flail mowers attached to an excavator arm. They can flatten broom that's grown to 4 metres, reach down slopes and up embankments and convert weeds to mulch on site. Follow up hand-pulling is generally required.

Cut and swab with herbicides

The only situation in which I will consider using herbicides is when dealing with woody weeds. For example, I recently had to remove a cork elm that was suckering profusely, with some suckers arising more than twice its height away from the trunk. If I had removed the top of the elm without poisoning the roots, the suckering would have increased. In another situation I had to remove cotoneaster and holly from a steep rocky hillside where they could not be grubbed. In the cut-and-swab method the herbicide is restricted to the target plant and by the time the woody trunk disintegrates there is little herbicide residue remaining.

I also participate in local bushland weed control, where I feel quite differently about herbicides. They are not in my immediate domestic environment or on my food, so I am more tolerant.

The cut-and-swab method involves cutting down the woody stem and immediately painting the stump with a mixture of herbicide and diesel or a wetting agent. It is critical to make the interval between cutting and painting as short as possible, as the plant will start to seal the wound within minutes of the cut. Another version of this technique is called 'drill and fill', where a hole is drilled into the cambium and herbicide is injected. The hole only needs to go just past the cambium layer to be absorbed (any deeper will use more herbicide for no extra effect). With large trunks, drill a number of holes about 15 centimetres apart and no more than 4 centimetres deep. It's only necessary to apply the herbicide to the exposed cambium when painting wounds because the heartwood is effectively dead. Remove shavings from the drill hole, as they will absorb the herbicide, making it ineffective.

Caution is still required because although these techniques restrict poison to the target, personal exposure can be quite high. I have seen cluttered and busy bushland worksites littered with open bottles of herbicide mixture and herbicide flicked around with a paintbrush. I prefer to use a laboratory squeeze bottle, which has a small opening and is made from chemical-resistant materials. I always use a face mask and protective gloves, overalls and boots.

Lawn weeds

Soils with low levels of calcium — especially those that don't break down organic matter quickly — are havens for dandelions, especially in lawns.

Clean mowers between jobs and mow before seed set to avoid spreading weeds.

Repair any spaces that develop within the lawn by first correcting soil (by aerating and adding compost and gypsum to compacted spots) and then use seed or runners to get desirable lawn plants established.

Single-species lawns are always more vulnerable to weeds, pests and disease. If the species selected succumbs to any problems, or has a seasonal period of low growth, weeds can become established. Multiple species are also more likely to cope with different environmental conditions: for instance, species that prefer sun or shade will become predominate in areas with those characteristics.

Tim's top six tips for keeping a weed free lawn

1. Feed the lawn with a certified organic lawn fertiliser so that it can compete with the weeds.
2. Mow often with a sharp-bladed mower. Mowing is particularly useful to prevent annual grasses from seeding. Use a catcher to remove seed.
3. Mow on a high setting and avoid 'scalping' at all cost — about 2 centimetres is low enough for a fine turf lawn and 2.5 to 3 centimetres for an all-purpose lawn.
4. Provide good drainage. Scarify and aerate at least once a year and install ag-drains in very wet spots.
5. Use hand-digging with a sharp knife or bulb digger. There are many useful digging tools — for example, hand forks or bulb diggers — but I find a good sturdy pocketknife is an excellent tool for lawn weeds. The blade can be used to dig, lever out and cut, depending on the size of the weed. If leaving a big hole, fill with compost or soil and sprinkle with lawn seed.
6. Use several grass species plus clover to keep the lawn healthy. Single-species lawns will generally have a period of the year when they are not growing optimally and are therefore susceptible to weed incursion.

Common lawn weeds and how to control them

Weed name	Description and control
Buttercup (*Ranunculus repens*)	Bright yellow flower in moist areas. Dig by hand.
Capeweed (*Arctotheca calendula*)	Yellow daisy-like flower with black centre. Dig before it produces seed and apply lime or dolomite.
Cat's ear (*Hypochaeris radicata*)	Hairy leaves and stem, multiple yellow flowers on one stalk. Dig or pull when soil is moist.
Creeping oxalis (*Oxalis corniculata*)	Clover-like leaf and small yellow flowers on a creeping stolon. Dig out.
Lawn daisy (*Bellis perennis*)	Pink and white flowers on an erect stem raising above fleshy leaves. Dig out.
Dandelion (*Taraxacum officinale*)	Rosette producing a single yellow daisy flower per hollow stem. Dig carefully to remove root.
Dock (*Rumex* species)	Large leaves and taproot with leaves and especially stems producing bronzed colours. Dig carefully to remove root.
Bindii is also called jo-jo(*Soliva sessilis*)	Fibrous root mass and many burrs. Tolerates mowing well. Dig before seed production.
Plantain (*Plantago lanceolata* or *P. major*)	Rosette with long, deeply veined leaves and tall erect flower spike with one dull green flower per stem. Dig carefully to remove root.
Mouse-ear chickweed (*Cerastium glomeratum*)	Mass of stems at the soil surface producing both leaves and roots and small white flowers in the spring and summer. Very difficult to pull. Must be dug out.
Nutgrass (*Cyperus rotundus*)	Grass-like plant with a triangular stem, very resistant to mowing. Dig carefully to remove the entire root.
Pearlwort (*Sagina procumbens*)	Very low dense rosettes with aggressive stolons. Dig carefully to remove root.

Stop weeds in their path
Many useful scraping tools can be applied to weeds that germinate between pavers or in cracks in pathways. An old knife or screwdriver or even a wire brush can be useful. I also use a stiff-bristled yard broom and a single blade from large tailor's scissors.

Flame or hot water is also ideal for use over paved areas, as are organic herbicides made from plant essential oils. Flame is particularly effective on gravel.

If using gravel, pebble or other mineral materials, it's best to lay them on a permeable agricultural fabric such as weed mat to stop weeds coming up from below.

Pasture weeds

Slashing is a good technique to prevent weeds from flowering and setting seeds. It's an ideal control method for annual grasses but is not very effective for plants with substantial underground reserves, such as bracken. Slashing early before flowering commences may prevent the plant from producing a seed stalk; slashing late may result in regrowth of a shorter stalk. Slashing after seed production may spread weed seeds.

If you graze stock, use high-density stocking rates for short periods to encourage the stock to eat broadleaf weeds such as capeweed and thistles. This will also help to reduce seed production from annual grasses. Perennial grasses are harder to control by grazing because they are often unattractive to stock and of low feed value. They may also have burrs that damage stock or stick in wool.

Non-palatable weeds can be made more palatable to stock by a spray with molasses in warm water, in a technique that provides organic growers with the same advantages that chemical users get from spray-topping pastures. Spray topping is the use of low doses of a hormone herbicide to sweeten plants and make them more attractive to grazing animals. Do ensure that non-palatable weeds are only a component of the daily diet and observe the stock to ensure they are not overgrazing on low-value weeds.

Try to avoid moving stock from weedy paddocks to clean areas when grasses are flowering.

Plough with tined or disc implements when pastures are re-sown. Discs cut the root systems more thoroughly but they also disturb soil more, so be prepared to follow up with some chipping or hand-pulling. If weeds are only scattered or infestations are small, hoeing or digging can be very effective.

You can use flame weeders or organic herbicides to remove broadleaf weeds at the rosette stage when they are ideal targets for these control methods. Smaller weeds require less attention, so start control early and plan to revisit the task several times.

3
Garden weeds

When weeding, the best way to make sure you are removing a weed and not a valuable plant is to pull on it. If it comes out of the ground easily, it is a valuable plant.

Anon

It is impossible to list here over 3,000 plants commonly called weeds in Australia. A selection of weeds has been chosen to reflect the wide range of possible plant types and management strategies, with emphasis on weeds that are widespread across the continent, or are serious weeds locally where they do occur. The control techniques suggested may also be applied to other weeds with a similar growth form or habit.

ANNUALS

Bathurst burr (*Xanthium spinosum*) is an annual that grows to about 1 metre. It has sharp, three-pronged yellow spines that it bears where the leaves emerge or stems branch. It can be dug out with care when young, but the stems are sharp and digging Bathurst burr is unpleasant. Always use gloves when handling Bathurst burr. Collect and burn mature plants with developed burrs.

Bathurst burr

Bindii or **jo-jo** (*Soliva sessilis*) is a spreading annual common in lawns and waste areas. If the infestation is not extensive it is easily dug out while young. Use a lawnmower to vacuum seed up — or alternatively use a household vacuum cleaner! A roll of foam sponge also works — just roll it across the lawn. The removal of seed as described works best in dry soils. Remember to clean the mower before using it on uninfected areas and place the dirty clippings in the middle of a hot compost heap or in the hard rubbish bin.

Buttercup (*Ranunculus repens*) is a winter-dominant annual with bright green foliage and small yellow flowers. Buttercup likes moist shady areas. It is poisonous to stock. It is easily pulled by hand or hoed when young, but makes a suitable groundcover for unused spaces and has pleasant flowers. Mature plants have an extensive root system and are hard to pull unless assisted by some digging or leverage from a garden fork. Use gloves — the natural plant oil from ranunculus may irritate skin.

Several yellow-flowered native plants are called buttercup, including some *Ranunculus* species. They look like *R. repens*, so careful identification is needed if there are native buttercups in your area.

Caltrop (*Tribulus terrestris*) is a summer-growing creeping ephemeral with a very sharp seed. People who know this plant will not be surprised to learn that the Latin original of caltrop means 'foot trap'. In military history a caltrop was a sharp pointed device that was thrown to the ground to disable cavalry horses or wheeled vehicles. Caltrop can be controlled by repeated cultivation. If burrs have formed, try to remove them by raking and burning to destroy seed. Use rolled-up sponge (available from rubber shops) to roll over infected lawns or other areas to collect seed or walk over the affected area in thongs!

Capeweed (*Arctotheca calendula*) is a common creeping weed of pasture, wasteland and sometimes gardens. It can be dug out at any time or severely reduced in extent and vigour by liming the soil. When digging, loosen the soil with a fork or other tool and extract as much taproot as possible. Graze capeweed-infected paddocks heavily during late winter and early spring, and establish vigorous clover and perennial grasses pasture.

> Capeweed is often mistaken for dandelion. It can be distinguished by its very pale and hairy leaf underside.

Cleavers or **goosegrass** or **goosefoot** (*Galium aparine*) has leaves and seeds that are covered in small hooked bristles that cleave to clothing or animal fur, thereby spreading the plant widely. It's a common garden weed, especially in reasonably fertile soils. It germinates early and can grow prostrate or will climb plants and rock walls. Exploit its readily breaking stems (the dispersal method) by handpicking (wear gloves) and carting it off to the compost heap. It has a lot of chlorophyll, trace elements and healthy cleavers has quite a lot of nitrogen. Mulch will prevent germination of cleavers.

It is suitable food for geese (as one of the common names implies) and other poultry and can be eaten by humans if cooked.

Cleavers is similar to three-horned bedstraw (*Galium tricornutum*). The burr-like prickly fruits of cleavers are held on short straight stalks. The fruit stalks of bedstraw are curved.

Cleavers almost made it into my list of useful weeds in Chapter 4, because it is easy to remove by hand. I encourage some cleavers in my garden as a cover crop and green manure plant. It can spread rapidly if not watched and controlled.

Cruciferous weeds include **wild radish** (*Raphanus raphanistrum*), **charlock** (*Sinapis arvensis*) and **turnip weed** (*Rapistrum rugosum*). They are mainly annuals but may grow as biennials under some conditions. Seed dispersal is by the action of wind, vehicles, animals and water. They are common weeds of fertile cultivated fields and wasteland, and in most situations gradually decline if the soil is not disturbed for a few seasons. The leaves and stalk of cruciferous weeds can be toxic to stock if eaten in large quantities, but the seed can be quite toxic also and can taint the flavour of milk and meat.

Cruciferous weeds may encourage the diseases of related crop and garden plants, such as the cabbage family, so keep them away from the vegetable garden. The stem of many crucifers is wrinkled just above the ground. This makes a weak point and the stem may break if pulled. Digging is better. Use a screwdriver in hard ground.

Discourage cruciferous weeds by applying fish emulsion, compost tea and liquid from your worm farm.

Fleabane is a serious weed of agriculture and wasteland. There are three fleabane species in Australia: flax leaf fleabane (*Conyza bonariensis*); Canadian fleabane (*Erigeron canadensis*); and tall fleabane (*Erigeron elatior*).

Fleabane contains volatile oils, tannic acid and gallic acid that may cause mucus and skin irritation in livestock or people. Horses are most susceptible, hence its American common name of 'horseweed'. Native Americans used it as an astringent and early settlers used it to treat diarrhoea and dysentery, and to repel fleas, hence its other common name. It is one of the few North American native plants to be a serious weed in Australia.

Some populations of fleabane are resistant to conventional herbicides, but can be treated with organic herbicide. If removing fleabane by hand, dispose of the seed heads by bagging or burning because seeds continue to mature when the plant is lopped.

Green amaranth (*Amaranthus viridis*) is easily controlled by hand-pulling or hoeing especially when small. It can produce large numbers of seeds so control it before seed sets or rogue larger plants. It is similar to **redroot amaranth** (*Amaranthus retroflexus*).

Groundsel (*Senecio vulgaris*) is a member of the daisy family. It is common in cultivated soil, tolerates a wide range of soil types and germinates readily throughout the year. It produces abundant wind-dispersed seed. Hoe young groundsel and pull out larger ones. Use a fork and trace and remove every root.

Uprooted plants may survive in humid conditions, so do not leave them on the soil surface. Mulch will prevent germination.

Mallow (*Malvia* species) is an annual but may become a perennial under some conditions. It is generally easily controlled by hoeing and hand-pulling but large infestations sometimes contain very large mature plants that need grubbing. The seeds of mallow are edible.

Noogoora burr (*Xanthium occidentale* and many alternative names, including *pungens*) is a shrub growing to 2.5 metres. It has a nasty thorn that contaminates wool and damages stock but it can be easily hoed before flowering. A rust fungus is known to be effective in southeast Queensland but has not established in other areas, possibly because there are multiple sub-species and species crosses of *X. strumarium*.

Pearlwort (*Sagina procumbens*) is an aggressive, low-growing annual that is quite susceptible to hand-pulling and digging. Because it is low growing it has potential as a cover crop plant, but it may be too aggressive for some gardeners. Can be a problem in lawns because it produces plentiful seed from very low growth.

Saffron thistle (*Carthamus lanatus*) grows to 1metre with multiple branches, each with a flower. It can be controlled with cultivation at an early stage (before formation of flowers).

Spurge comes in many types, both weedy and cultivated varieties, but perhaps the most common weedy version is petty spurge (*Euphorbia peplus*). Spurge thrives in cultivated soil and makes rapid growth over a short life cycle, producing long-lived seeds. Spurge is a good target for hand-weeding or hoeing, as it is a soft weed that easily releases from the ground. Spurge stems release milky latex when broken that can irritate the skin and produce an allergic reaction in some people. Use gloves and if working on larger *Euphorbia* species use eye protection (the latex can be quite painful if it gets into eyes or mucous tissues). Spurge is another weed that I tolerate in the garden as a small component of the weed mix and as fuel for the compost heap. Grasp carefully at ground level and pull to remove as much root as possible.

Thorn apple (*Datura stramonium*) is a vigorously growing shrub that reaches to about 1 metre. It is poisonous to stock and people. Plants should be dug out and destroyed.

Three-cornered Jack (*Emex australis*), also known as **spiny emex**, produces nasty prickly seeds that hitch a ride on animal fur or attach to the rubber soles of thongs and shoes. It can be hand-pulled or cultivated before seeding during winter. Summer cultivation may encourage the plant to produce seed. Use rolled-up foam sheets to roll over infected areas and collect seed (that should then be burned). A light spray with organic herbicide at the time when seed is maturing may prevent seed from setting.

Variegated thistle (*Silybum marianum*), also called **spotted thistle**, can be controlled by mowing or cultivation prior to flowering if followed by establishment of pasture or cover-crops. Variegated thistle may cause poisoning of stock in certain conditions.

Wild radish (*Raphanus raphanistrum*) is an annual that will sometimes grow as a biennial. Seed disperses by wind and animals. It's a weed of cereal crops and wasteland, and may be toxic to stock. Because of the cereal connection, wild radish seed sometimes arrives in meadow hay or mulching straw. Wild radish prefers soils that are low in calcium, phosphate and manganese. Organic matter and adjustment of soil nutrients will greatly assist other control measures. Use compost additions and compost tea. Hoe seedlings when they are young and pull older plants. The root must be severed below the crown root swelling.

Wireweed (*Polygonum aviculare*), also known as **hogweed**, grows through spring, summer and autumn. It has a prostrate habit but will also ramble or climb over other plants. It's easily pulled or hoed from moist soil especially when small.

Annual grasses

Barleygrass (*Hordeum glaucum*) is a common winter-growing bunching grass that reaches to about 30 centimetres.

Barnyard grass (*Echinochloa crus-galli*) is a summer annual growing to about 50 to 100 centimetres.

Ryegrass (*Lolium* species) appears in both annual and perennial versions and is a common garden weed. Ryegrass pollen is a common cause of allergy.

Summer grass (*Digitaria sanguinalis*) forms small tufts from a creeping stem. It grows in summer and roots readily from nodes.

Wild oats (*Avena* species) is a common weed of gardens and lawns.

Winter grass (*Poa annua*) is a weed of lawns, paths and cultivated areas in winter. It can produce seed while growing very low.

General advice for control of annual grasses

Control annual grasses by mowing, hand-pulling or cultivation. Where weeds are grass-dominant, add calcium, compost and compost tea. Some grasses, such as barnyard grass, have fleshy roots that should be completely removed. Do not let annual grasses produce seed. Mow, brush-cut or pull plants before they produce seed and mulch bare soil to stop germination and growth. Annual grasses will necessarily disappear if seed is not renewed.

BIENNIALS

Blackberry nightshade (*Solanum nigrum*) grows from 50 to 90 centimetres in height and is identified by its branching habit and small black berries. It is susceptible to pulling or hoeing when small. Control it before seed is set, if possible. Nightshade may harbour diseases of *Solanum* crop plants such as tomato, capsicum, eggplant and potato.

Fennel (*Foeniculum vulgare*) is a tall, erect plant growing to 2 metres that smells like aniseed. Fennel should be pulled from the soil and the roots allowed to thoroughly dry out. Larger plants may require a mattock. The swollen stem base may be eaten raw or cooked.

Salvation Jane or **Paterson's curse** (*Echium plantagineum*) was introduced to Australia by John McArthur in 1843 and was first recorded as a weed at Mr Paterson's property near Albury in 1880. It is originally from the Mediterranean region but now occurs in all Australian states.

Salvation Jane can be controlled with digging or cultivation before seed set, and by hand-pulling. Remove as much taproot as possible and follow up with established pasture, cover crops or appropriate crop rotation. Seven biological control agents have been released for salvation Jane.

PERENNIALS

Artichoke thistle (*Cynara cardunculus*) is susceptible to repeated cultivation. Cut the seed heads off before seed matures and grub out as much taproot as possible. Very young seedlings do not compete well with dense pasture or cover crop.

Bidgee-widgee (*Acaena anserinifolia*) is a perennial with a woody rootstock. It can be pulled, ideally before seed set. Collect mature seed heads and burn them.

Blackberries (*Rubus fruticosus*) are pernicious weeds of bushland, especially in wet gullies and alongside streams, but also persistent in dry areas and wasteland. Seeds are widely dispersed by birds and foxes and they can self-layer from root tips. They must be cut down and dug out. My preferred tool is a mattock and they lift surprisingly easily if the soil is in good condition. Wear gloves and overalls, as well as sunglasses to protect your eyes. (See also Chapter 5, Environmental weeds.)

Boxthorn or **African boxthorn** (*Lycium ferocissimum*) is a spiny plant growing to 5 metres and originally introduced as a hedge plant. It spreads by seed (bird and fox), so control should be focused on the period before seed production. Small plants can be grubbed using a mattock or other tools. It can be cut or pulled effectively if larger roots are also completely pulled from the soil. Larger bushes can be removed with a tree-popper, car winch or chain and tractor. Cultivate soil or pull seedlings in the next few seasons to prevent re-establishment. Establish vigorous pasture or native plants to provide competition for new plants.

Bracken fern (*Pteridium esculentum*) has thick scaly rhizomes that give rise to new growth in spring and summer. Bracken can be toxic to stock. Slashing and competition from strong-growing pasture will help to control it. Ensure soils are well supplied with potassium to reduce the competitive pressure from bracken. Pigs will root up the rhizomes and eat them.

California thistle (*Cirsium californicum*) is not susceptible to digging or hand-pulling unless it is very thorough. Very young seedlings do not compete well with dense pasture or cover crop so use plant competition to reduce germination of California thistle. A mature patch of California thistle can be quite allelopathic to pasture plants and other types of thistles.

Note: Cirsium thistles may hybridise easily and there may be many crosses.

Camphor laurel (*Cinnamomum camphora*) is a fast-growing tree to more than 30 metres. It spreads by seed and by suckering. The wood is aromatic with camphor, which ensures that it has few insect pests. The camphor also delays the composting process. The tree should be felled and the roots grubbed.

Canada thistle (*Cirsium arvense*) is a very invasive herbaceous perennial weed that grows vertical shoots from lateral roots. It grows readily from small pieces of root and also produces masses of seed that can live for 20 years or more in the soil. Canada thistle is also known as **creeping thistle** because of its ability to grow a very extensive and deep lateral root system. The roots are edible. Only significant shading out with very competitive crop or groundcover plants, or very extensive digging, can control Canada thistle once it is established. Careful monitoring and immediate action is required if this weed is known in your district.

Castor oil plant (*Ricinus communis*) is a member of the spurge family, Euphorbiaceae. It is a perennial shrub growing to 2 metres with large palmate (palm-like) leaves. It can also grow as an annual in some situations. It is poisonous to stock and can cause allergy and skin reactions in humans. It can be grubbed but the toxic seeds should be collected and destroyed. Large roots must be removed. Use gloves and eye protection.

One-leaf Cape tulip (*Homeria breyniana*) and **two-leaf Cape tulip** (*H. miniata*) may be controlled by repeated cultivation or digging. Cultivate before production of seed and follow with the establishment of vigorous pasture, native shrubs or appropriate crop rotation. Digging may need to be deep (down to 30 centimetres).

Dock (*Rumex* species) is common in cultivated soil or waste ground but the most common is **broad-leaved dock** (*Rumex obtusifolius*). Dock can produce many seeds, perhaps 30,000 to 50,000 per plant, and the seeds are very long-lived (20 years). Dock dies down to reddish stems in the summer.

Dock cannot be hoed once the taproot develops because it will re-grow, even from pieces of root left deep in the soil. It can be dug out with a mattock, or a special dock digger, but any pieces of root the size of your little finger must be removed to a depth of 15 centimetres. Slash mature plants to stop or reduce the quantity of seed production. Pull the seedlings while small. Dock moth (*Chamaesphecia doryliformis*) from Morocco is available for biological control.

Where dock is dominant, add calcium, compost or compost tea, and consider aerating soil.

Field bindweed (*Convolvulus arvensis*) is a low summer-growing noxious and persistent weed with a widely branched rhizome root system. It must be carefully dug to remove as much rhizome as possible.

Fishbone fern (*Nephrolepis cordifolia*) is a common fern with fronds to 1 metre tall and thick scaly roots and tubers. You must remove as much root and tuber as possible. Due to the dense growth, digging can be difficult.

Gorse or **furse** (*Ulex europaeus*) bushes should be removed by chaining or grubbing and then burned. Some repeated hoeing may be necessary to remove seedlings. Seedlings to 30 centimetres can be pulled.

Guildford grass (*Romulea rosea*), also called **onion grass** or **nut grass**, is a South African native that is widespread across southern Australia in gardens, pastures and roadsides. It likes compacted ground. Guildford grass prefers high rainfall, compacted ground with poor drainage, low organic matter, low calcium and high magnesium soils. It can cause fibre balls in the bowels of cattle, sheep and horses and may also cause infertility in stock. Compacted soil should be loosened with a fork or other aerating tools to incorporate oxygen into soil.

Dig the corms carefully to remove as much of the underground material as possible. The incidence of Guildford grass usually drops off significantly once soil condition improves.

Horehound (*Marrubium vulgare*) can form thick infestations but is easy to pull or grab from the soil. It responds well to slashing or grazing but the root must be removed. Stock should not eat too much horehound because it can cause liver damage. For larger infestations, burn to remove the stems and kill the plentiful seed. Follow up with cultivation of seedlings and then plant pasture or a smother crop.

Horehound is used to make beer and is an excellent herb for warding off colds and flu if it is taken as soon as symptoms are first noticed. Infuse just two or three small leaves in a mug of boiled water several times a day. Beware of strong doses as it can also damage human livers.

Khaki weed (*Alternanthera repens*) is a low-growing creeping weed that roots readily from nodes and forms thick matted growth. It can be pulled or hoed and any mature burrs should be removed and burned.

Morning glory (*Ipomoea indica*) is a vigorous trailing vine that readily climbs over anything in its path. There are ornamental garden varieties that are much less vigorous. Slash the tops and dig the roots. Be careful with removed material as it roots easily from stems. Roots of morning glory may penetrate 5 metres into the soil, but only surface roots to 1 metre or less are capable of re-growing.

Nutgrass (*Cyperus rotundus*), also sometimes called **nutsedge**, **purple nutgrass** or **purple nutsedge**, is a sedge. It is also a difficult and spreading weed known for its invasiveness in more than 90 countries. It is not susceptible to cultivation or hand-pulling, so thorough and repeated action is required to have much effect. It is attractive to the long-billed corella (*Cacatua tenuirostris*), which will help to control spread of the weed. The tuber can be eaten by humans, although it is bitter in taste.

Either remove as much root as possible or leave tubers exposed at the surface to dry out. Cultivate at least once every fortnight until it's removed. Nutgrass may be susceptible to the black plastic method if tubers are not very deep.

Onion weed (*Asphodelus fistulosus*) can be hand-pulled or cultivated repeatedly before flowering. Treated areas should be planted to out-compete with the regrowth.

Oxalis species are serious weeds of gardens and waste areas.

Creeping oxalis (*Oxalis corniculata*) can grow as either an annual or a perennial. Unlike other oxalis, it spreads only by seed and not by bulbils or tubers. Because of its growth habit it is the easiest oxalis to control and hand forking is adequate but this should be achieved before seed matures. Note that the Australian native *O. perennans* has the same common name.

Pink-flowered oxalis (*Oxalis corymbosa*) grows quickly, competes well and may spread by combination of bulbils, seed and stolons. The underground parts break easily if pulled, although in good soil conditions they can be 'traced' and removed by carefully following the small white roots with a good trowel or special weeding tool.

Soursob (*Oxalis pes-caprae*) was introduced into South Australia in 1839 (or soon after) and listed in a Hackney nursery catalogue published in the *Adelaide Observer* on 3 May 1845. By 1879 the plant was recognised by botanist Richard Schomburgh as a bad weed in gardens and wheat crops.

Soursob can be pulled in the home garden, but requires careful and persistent attention. Frequent pulling is fine, but digging is best. The most effective time will be what is called 'bulb exhaustion' stage, when the old bulbs are spent and the new bulbils are just formed and very small. Bulb exhaustion can be identified because a

Garden weeds

Soursob

significant percentage the old bulbs become flaky and empty, and if pressed between thumb and forefinger, can be rubbed apart. If the soil is in good condition, a significant number of the new bulbils can be pulled out with the roots. Grip the plant close to the ground and pull, gently but firmly.

By the time oxalis has produced flowers it will already have produced a crop of new bulbs. Although they may still be small, they tend to point straight up. Their connection with the root is brittle, so they easily snag and fall off. It is best to pull oxalis early, before the new bulbs are formed.

> Mulch is seldom useful for soursob — it will grow through all but the deepest and most continuous barrier. I once put a very large compost pile on top of some soursob bulbs; one bulb was able to produce a strong shoot that grew through almost 120 centimetres of compost, to eventually produce one of the healthiest oxalis plants you could ever see! Multiple layers of paper or cardboard may be effective at eliminating some bulbs, but unfortunately some bulbs will simply become dormant and wait for the following season to germinate. It is not widely appreciated that many plants arising from underground parts do not need to grow every year. In fact, it provides survival advantage if some do not grow in any one season because they wait for better conditions. Ever wondered why some years the display of native orchids is so much better than others? The orchid exhibits very well this practice of not all germinating in each year.

Because of the brittleness, some stems will break, leaving old and new bulbs behind. The plant will be weakened, however. Remove as much of the top growth as possible — this will prevent moisture and nutrients from being reabsorbed by the bulb. Even when the plant breaks, with a bit of luck the bulb will be dragged closer to the surface, making it easier to get at next time around.

Dig with a hand fork to get under the bulbs. Work the fork gently under the bulbs while gripping the tops and pull them away. Use both a gentle tugging and digging action.

The worst problem is where bulbs grow through the roots of garden plants, causing the bulbils to get hooked off as the root is pulled through. In this situation, constant pulling is required to weaken the new plant before the bulbils can acquire new energy from photosynthesis.

Soursob can produce a large fleshy tuber. This is a storage organ only and soursob does not grow from the tuber alone. If a bulb remains attached to the tuber when the tops have been pulled, it may still be able to get access to food in the tuber. There may also be a bulb attached below the tuber, ready to grow away.

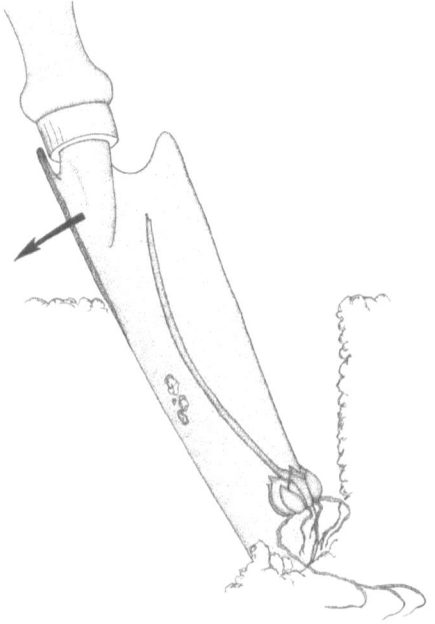

Position the trowel underneath bulbs

Soursob will keep grassy weeds at bay. Because the stems are succulent and die away in summer, it reduces the summer fire-fuel load. This leads some organic viticulturists and orchardists to encourage soursob in the immediate area under the vine or drip line of trees.

Pampas grass (*Cortaderia selloana*) is a tall grass growing to 4 metres with large plumed seed heads. It produces prolific seed and can be a serious fire hazard. Pampas is extremely difficult to dig because of its very dense growth habit. Cut down to the ground and remove large infestations with heavy machinery, such as a bobcat or excavator, or make a bonfire on top to burn the roots.

Periwinkle (*Vinca major*) and the **lesser periwinkle** (*V. minor*) are invasive rambling weeds especially around creeks and in damp areas. It is not controlled by mowing or mulching and must be dug out to remove all the underground parts.

Prickly pear (*Opuntia* species) is a succulent perennial that arrived in Australia with the First Fleet and grew to become a major weed in Queensland. Biological controls are available. If removing by hand or mechanical means, ensure that the root system is removed with no parts left in the soil. Prickly pear fruits are delicious to eat and culinary versions are available. They should not be planted near creeks or bushland where they can escape.

Privet (*Ligustrum lucidum*) produces many small black seeds that are dispersed by birds. Privet pollen may also contribute to hay fever. Rake up fallen berries and remove to the compost to prevent birds eating them. Check under bird roosts for young seedlings and hoe or pull them before they become large. Hand-pull seedlings and grub larger plants, removing any surface roots. Ringbark larger plants.

Ragwort (*Senecio jacobaea*) is a tall biennial or perennial weed that produces large quantities of wind-dispersed seeds. Two beetles, *Chrysolina hyperici* and *C. quadrigemina,* were released in Victoria in the 1930s. The beetles have low mobility so it is best to collect branches from infected plants and attach them to plants you want to control.

Rhus tree or **sumac** (*Toxicodendron succedaneum*) is a small deciduous tree to 5 metres. It can be controlled by ringbarking but the roots should be grubbed to prevent suckering.

Silver-leaf nightshade (*Solanum elaeagnifolium*): See **blackberry nightshade** and control in the same way.

Skeleton weed (*Chondrilla juncea*) has a deep taproot growing to a metre or more. It exudes a milky latex when stems are broken. Skeleton weed is not susceptible to cultivation and when digging take care to not distribute pieces of the root because they grow readily. Planting out with competitive plants can help control it, and improving nitrogen and phosphorous levels will reduce its growth but not eradicate it.

Prevent skeleton weed from seeding if possible. Use a lower dose of organic herbicide or vinegar to prevent seed from setting. A rust fungus was released in 1971 and significantly controlled the narrow-leaf form. Unfortunately, the broadleaf form is not susceptible and has largely taken over the same territory.

Sorrel (*Rumex acetosella*) is a prostrate spreading weed with very extensive lateral roots. Sorrel can be dug but the delicate roots break easily and must be carefully traced and removed if digging is to be effective. Add lime or dolomite to soils infested with sorrel and increase air penetration by working a fork into the soil (no need to turn the soil over).

Hoeing is not an ideal control because of the extensive root system, but it will work if repeated regularly. Mulching is ineffective and mulch often increases the growth and extent of spread.

St John's wort (*Hypericum perforatum*) is a yellow-flowered perennial herb that grows from creeping rhizomes and windblown seed. It can be controlled by deep cultivation followed by establishment of a competitive plant cover.

There are native Australian *Hypericum*, so establish identification carefully before controlling in bushland.

Three-corner garlic (*Allium triquetrum*) has small white bulbs and a triangular leaf. It can form very dense colonies, especially in grassland and under shade. In agricultural settings it has the potential to taint milk. Mulching is ineffective unless a complete and thick barrier can be maintained for several seasons, but the bulbs are often quite shallow and it is easily pulled. Extreme care should be taken with the bulbs, as they are very resistant to composting or fermentation.

Tree-of-heaven (*Ailanthus altissima*) grows to 18 metres. It is poisonous to stock and causes a dermatitis reaction in some people. The tree should be felled and the root system grubbed out.

Wandering Jew (*Tradescantia albiflora*) is a succulent creeping perennial that roots easily from each node. It can be a very invasive weed especially in moist shady locations. To remove it, pull the plant and dig the roots. Beware of pulled or dug plants, as they will root easily in moist weather. Put them into the centre of a hot compost or leave them to dry out on a path, or partially ferment them in a plastic bag before adding to the compost.

Perennial grasses

Creeping bent grass (*Agrostis stolonifera*) and **red fescue** (*Festuca rubra*) are summer–autumn lawn grasses that readily escape to become weedy elsewhere in the garden. They grow rapidly and spread by stolons. They produce long-lasting seeds. These grasses can be hoed when young, but this is much more difficult if they are mixed in with crop plants, due to the stolons. Remove every bit of stolon by hand and prevent lawn grasses from producing seed.

African lovegrass (*Eragrostis curvula*) is a noxious weed in some states. It deserves special attention to remove it from all cultivated areas because it's very competitive and will severely inhibit less aggressive plants. Use repeated mowing or brush-cutting to remove as much top growth as possible. Follow up cutting with an organic herbicide.

Couch grass (*Agropyron repens*) is a problematic stoloniferous grassy weed, often finding its way into gardens, cultivated paddocks, vineyards and waste ground. It can produce very long rhizomes and multiple nodes.

Mow, hoe and burn to reduce vigour, but you will not eradicate couch without significant digging to remove all underground parts or by using solarisation or the black plastic method. Digging is ineffective unless all the roots are removed from the soil and this risks spreading couch further. Dig carefully to avoid breaking the rhizomes. Loosen the soil in front with a fork (to avoid chopping roots) and pull out pieces as large as you can manage. Sometimes couch will be quite shallowly rooted and you can dig underneath, rolling a large piece of turf over. Shake out excess soil and bury deep in very hot compost, or leave rhizomes in the full sun to dry out thoroughly before composting.

Couch can be limited to lawns by barriers, but physical barriers need to be quite deep in fertile soils and edges will need to be trimmed as the rhizomes are persistent. Plant barriers utilising densely growing plants also work. Try cannas (*Canna* species), red-hot pokers (*Kniphofia uvaria*) or comfrey (*Symphytum officinale*).

Feather grass or **feather top** (*Pennisetum villosum*) forms dense and compact tufts. It is similar to **fountain grass** (*Pennisetum setaceum*) and both are persistent. Small tufts should be grubbed and the regrowth flamed or treated with an organic herbicide.

Johnson grass (*Sorghum halepense*) is a very tall, fast-growing grass. Control is only possible by removing every piece of rhizome.

Paspalum (*Paspalum dilatatum*) is a lawn weed and is often found growing under the drip line in orchards. Paspalum can be very difficult to dig during the main growing season, but is easily lifted at other times. Use a mattock for large clumps.

Perennial ryegrass (*Lolium perenne*) is easily controlled by hand-pulling or hoeing if it is in small clumps only. Larger areas should be mowed to reduce seed production.

Slugs and snails and weeds

If you have lots of weeds, you may have trouble with slugs and snails. Try the following:
- mow or cultivate around sensitive plants. A barrier of several mower widths will reduce slug and snail attack

- use hardwood wood shavings as a barrier around sensitive plants
- use a mulch of shredded mullein, wormwood, southernwood, basil, rue or rosemary leaves and twigs. They all repel slugs and snails
- spray an extract of wormwood, ivy, white hellebore, quassia, lime, garlic and chilli, neem or rotenone directly on feeding snails or as a barrier spray
- use alum (aluminium sulphate), copper sulphate or copper silicate sprays as a barrier
- purchase iron chelate baits or copper silicate sprays from a garden centre
- use beer traps or any other fermenting substance such as port wine, Vegemite or common yeast. Sink the traps into the ground at 1-metre spacings between the garden and snail refuge areas and change them every week or 10 days. Added cornflour makes them extra sticky.

4
Good weeds

A plant whose virtues have not yet been discovered
Emerson

Weeds come uninvited into the garden, but they need not necessarily be unwelcome visitors. They may bring multiple beneficial functions. Weeds protect soil from erosion by wind and rain and runoff. By keeping soil friable and permeable, and by slowing the rate of flow of surface water, weeds recharge soil moisture.

Weeds are also indicators of soil condition. There will always be weeds, but the particular weeds that establish on a site are the result of many factors (including the invasion of seed and vegetative growing parts) but also upon the particular soil and climatic conditions that operate at that location. For example, sorrel and dock are indicators of acid soil; dock may also thrive where soil is compacted and waterlogged. Bracken really takes over where nitrogen is low, whereas nettles, fat hen and sow thistles prefer fertile soil with sufficient nitrogen.

Weeds do not only protect soil from erosion — they build and renew soil. Deep roots open up soil spaces, and feeding roots shed organic matter and leak exudates that encourage soil biology. They combine with symbiotic and dependent organisms to form a rhizosphere around the roots that becomes a habitat for many other organisms. It effectively creates an environment potentially as biologically complex as a rainforest. Healthy soil is by no means just a soil with adequate organic matter; really healthy soil can *only* develop where plant roots are present. Deep-rooted weeds bring up minerals from deep in the soil and all weeds capture and recycle nutrients that might otherwise be lost. If you pull or chop weeds and recycle them via the compost, you can enhance the return of minerals to the garden. Grasses and some taproot weeds are capable of breaking up hard soil pans.

And some weeds are not just edible — they're positively delicious and healthful. Bitter greens such as dandelion are an excellent example of a useful dietary supplement available from the garden with no cost and minimal tending. We allow a few edible weeds to flower and produce seed each year to maintain a self-replacing population at a controllable level.

WEEDS AS INDICATORS OF SOIL CONDITION

Weeds indicate soil condition. Legumes, including vetch and clover, are able to fix nitrogen from air in the soil spaces. They flourish where nitrogen is low and gradually improve the soil they grow in. Sorrel thrives where soil is acidic and low in calcium, so an abundance of sorrel is a pretty good indication that the pH needs to be raised. Adding lime, dolomite and seaweed meal would achieve this. In fact, gardeners with discerning palates can use sorrel to compare soils — the more bitter the sorrel tastes the lower the pH of the soil (it is edible and quite safe in the quantities that can be hand harvested). Fumitory, chickweed, cleavers, sow thistle, nettles and fat hen indicate fertile soils that are well supplied with nutrients and adequate nitrogen.

So, the particular weeds that a soil supports will be an indication of conditions within the soil, including nutrients, pH and friability, as well as depth and moisture supply. But the weeds will inevitably alter the soil condition over time, and many weeds, especially the ones in this chapter, will actually improve soil and repair the deficiencies that led to that particular weed becoming established in the first place. The legumes mentioned above gradually build soil nitrogen, and the deep-rooted plants mine nutrients from low in the soil profile and return them to the surface layer. The deep taproot weeds are particularly useful for this purpose. I used to hate dock with a vengeance until I learned not to bother trying to pull or dig it in dry conditions. When soil is moist, dock comes away easily with a little levering with a mattock or dock digger. Remove seeds by roguing beforehand and pull seedlings emerging afterwards while they are still small. Docks particularly concentrate potassium, iron and copper. Spurge mines the soil for boron, yarrow accumulates phosphorous, copper, potassium and calcium and horsetail collects silica, cobalt and calcium.

WEEDS AND BIODIVERSITY

Weeds are part of the diversity of living things. Although they may seriously detract from local biodiversity, they can also augment it. Weeds can damage local biodiversity by invading native vegetation and crowding indigenous plants out. They can benefit biodiversity by providing food and habitat for native animals and by preventing erosion and silting up of waterways.

Many of the beneficial predatory insects that are encouraged to use the garden

DON'T LET GARDEN PLANTS INVADE BUSHLAND

Bushland requires special protection from weeds. Select garden plants that do not threaten native bush near you. If you have plants that may escape into the wild, use strategies to control them, such as removing flowers or fruit by trimming, or by fencing or netting to prevent access by birds and animals that will distribute them in dung or on fur or feathers.

by the presence of flowering weeds are indigenous or Australian species. Flowering weeds also attract useful native pollinators such as butterflies. By selectively weeding to leave in place some of the easier to control and more useful weeds, areas of the garden we previously thought of as unproductive wasteland now become very useful. Daisy bushes, *Alyssum* and *Ageratum,* for instance, are introduced plants but are attractive to many native insects and provide useful quantities of pollen and nectar. Use them to occupy wild or undeveloped parts of the garden and keep less attractive and beneficial weeds at bay.

Using natives as groundcovers

There are many native plants that make great groundcovers, including edible species such as purslane and pigface. Here is a list of just a few native groundcovers.

Purslane (*Portulaca oleracea*) is edible and low growing (see more details on page 172).

Swainsonia including **Sturt's desert pea** (*Swainsona formosa*) is a low, creeping, drought-hardy legume especially suited to full sun and dry conditions.

Fan flowers (*Scaevola* species) are attractive, low-growing, drought-hardy plants that grow to a height of 15 to 30 centimetres and bear white, blue or purple flowers. There are over 70 Australian species. Fan flowers are especially suited to full sun and dry conditions.

Button everlasting daisy (*Helichrysum scorpioides*) and other species are a colourful and drought-hardy low groundcover.

Running postman (*Kennedia prostrata*) is a very useful leguminous groundcover. It is drought tolerant but may become a little sparse in dry situations. In suitable soils it makes a dense groundcover. It prefers lighter soils and a sunny position.

Rice flower (*Pimelea* species) is not to be confused with the taller-growing rice flower from the genus *Ozothamnus*. Pimelea remains low growing, especially the New Zealand native *Pimelea prostrata*.

Native grasses

Kangaroo grass (*Themeda triandra*), **wallaby grass** (*Austrodanthonia* species), **tussock grasses** (*Poa* species) and **spear grass** (*Austrostipa* species) are all low-maintenance plants with a low water requirement. Their flowers attract native butterflies and birds.

GETTING THE BALANCE RIGHT

Every gardener needs to discover for themselves how to transform a general understanding about the potential benefits of weeds into a practical system for their particular circumstances.

Organic gardeners should cultivate their observation skills, making notes or taking photographs to aid memory. For instance, in the age of mobile phones and cheap digital cameras, it is easy to build a photo library containing images of very young weed seedlings. Use these to identify what they grow into and to learn to recognise the very early growth stage so that you can selectively pull out or hoe the ones you really don't want.

It takes a while to know how many dandelion or purslane you should allow to go to seed to ensure regeneration without them taking over. It also takes time to get really proficient with use of a scuffle hoe, but it is worth persisting.

As we have seen in Chapter 1, garden or crop plants can easily become weeds and weeds can contribute positive benefits, but they still need to be controlled.

Jerusalem artichoke (*Helianthus tuberosus*) is a welcome food plant in my garden. It also has potential as a weed barrier for limiting invasion by less productive weeds, but it can easily escape and needs to be checked. I control it by growing it in very large pots (not very effective), growing it inside a partly buried old tractor tyre (much more effective) and by pulling them up. Pulled tops are an excellent compost ingredient but the tubers will grow in all but the hottest compost heap. The tubers are eaten, given away or sent to the hard rubbish dump as a last resort. As I travel a great deal,

I occasionally return home to find a neglected garden and spend some time digging artichoke tubers. I have, however, kept the artichoke patch small enough that I am not overwhelmed.

Areas of my Stirling garden that were reclaimed from serious weed infestation are now planted with space-occupying shrubs such as *Echium* species, daisies and pelargonium. These plants spread well, have a long flowering season, provide beneficial insect habitat, compete well against regrowth weeds and I can easily move them if I want to redevelop that area later. In fact, even if I redevelop the area later with a more permanent use in mind, these species will survive being dug up and relocated, and they grow easily from cuttings or seed.

Good annuals

Borage (*Borago officinalis*) is an attractive annual that has edible flowers and leaves. The flowers look great in salads and leaves can be cooked in soups or mixed with cabbage and steamed. Rogue the developing seed heads to prevent it from spreading too widely. Borage fits well into any small open spaces in the garden, such as spots left by a failed tomato plant.

Chickweed (*Stellaria media*) is a prostrate, spreading weed with white flowers. Young plants are easily hoed and plants of any age are easily pulled. Chickweed makes excellent chicken feed, but is also edible for humans, raw or cooked. Prevent chickweed from setting seed to limit its distribution. Keep it away from the greenhouse because it may host whitefly and red-legged earth mite. For hand pulling, use fingers to scratch into soil and remove the small, shallow fibrous roots.

Cress, including **shepherd's purse** (*Capsella bursa-pastoris*), **hairy cress** (*Cardamine hirsuta*) and others, are rapid growing and generally small, providing little competition. **Garden cress** (*Lepidium sativum*) is the most succulent but they are all edible. Cress produces masses of long-lived seed. As the seeds are many and small, control spread of this weed by preventing seed set, mulch and/or frequent light hoeing.

Fat hen (*Chenopodium album*) also called **lambsquarters** grows through much of the year but flowers in summer. It is an edible weed that is common on fertile soil. It almost made it into my list of undesirable weeds because it seeds extensively and can take over, but it is relatively easy to hoe when small or to pull when larger. In ideal sites it can become very tall, perhaps reaching several metres. It makes an excellent addition to the compost heap. Break up larger stems before composting. Fat hen develops a strong root system that helps to build soil humus and is a soil improver. It is edible in salads when young and as a substitute for spinach when older. Fat hen does not handle constant mowing.

Forget-me-not (*Myosotis arvensis*) is a summer-growing annual reaching 30 to 60 centimetres in height. It is very persistent but fortunately is easily pulled or hoed. It produces masses of attractive bright-blue flowers. The seeds stick to animals and clothes.

Fumitory (*Fumaria* species) is an annual sprawling weed that rambles over other plants but is easily pulled and makes excellent compost. Fumitory stems tend to be very brittle just above the soil surface. I pull fumitory by 'winding up' the stems. Using this action, wrapping the fumitory around your wrist, rather like coiling a rope, it's possible to remove huge quantities of the weed quickly over a large area with minimal effort. The broken stem butts that remain attached to the soil are then plucked in a separate pass. Left unchecked, fumitory will smother many other plants, so it should be pulled before seed set. However, because of its rambling growth habit it makes an excellent smother crop in later winter.

Nasturtium (*Tropaeolum majus*) is a fast-growing, rambling, long-flowering, brightly coloured annual from Peru. It grows in any sunny, well-drained position. Leaves and flowers can be used in salads. They have a peppery taste. Nasturtium produces plenty of seed and will come up where not wanted, but is easily pulled.

They are excellent for covering any unsightly areas in the garden. The green seeds are a substitute for capers.

Pennyroyal (*Mentha pulegium*) is a spreading prostrate herb in the mint family. Some gardeners use pennyroyal as a cover crop because it stays very low, produces a lovely spearmint aroma when walked upon or crushed and has both culinary and medicinal uses. It is susceptible to hoeing but care should be taken to remove as much root material as possible as it regenerates easily from nodes on the root or stem. Like many other medicinal and culinary herbs, pennyroyal should be treated with caution as a culinary herb or infusion and used in small doses only — the essential oils can become toxic in larger doses.

Purslane or **pigweed** (*Portulaca oleracea*) is a succulent found all over the world. The seeds, fleshy green leaves and red or yellow stems can be eaten, although superior cultivars are much tastier than the common garden weed, which is quite sour. Indigenous Australians used the seed and leaves as food. It is low spreading, making it an excellent cover crop under vegetables. It is also easily pulled from moist soil, mulch stops it from germinating and chickens love it. The sour taste is due to higher levels of omega-3 fatty acids, alpha-tocopherol, alpha-linolenic acid, ascorbic acid, beta-carotene and glutathione.

Scarlet pimpernel (*Anagallis arvensis*) is too small and low growing to be a serious weed. It has pleasant red flowers and grows rapidly, covering bare soil. It produces masses of long-lived seed, so remove some tops each year to limit seed production. It is easily controlled by hand-pulling and hoeing.

Shepherd's purse (*Capsella bursa-pastoris*) has a slender taproot and provides many of the benefits of dandelion, but is less useful because it is an annual and it is not as esculent. Pull tops before they flower to limit seed production.

Sow thistle (*Sonchus oleraceus*), also called **milk thistle**, is a common garden weed that likes cultivated soil and any unused corner. It grows rapidly and produces a lot of seed that is easily dispersed by wind. Sow thistle provides good groundcover and nectar for beneficial insects. It produces a milky white juice from broken stems and leaves, which may irritate some people. Use gloves when pulling. It is easily controlled by cultural methods. Hoe young seedlings or hand-pull carefully to remove the crown root. Break up roots and flowers and compost them. Stems can be left as mulch. Young sow thistle leaves are one of my favourite garden weeds for eating when used as a salad vegetable.

Stinging nettle (*Urtica urens*) is an erect annual weed that grows to 60 centimetres. It should not be confused with the perennial *Urtica dioica*. Cultivate or hand-pull but use gloves. Annual stinging nettle has similar properties to the perennial version and can be substituted in the recipes given below for *U. dioica*.

Valerian (*Valeriana officinalis*), also called **garden heliotrope**, is an attractive plant with a long flowering period and flowers that attract beneficial insects. It is easily pulled by hand at any time and young seedlings can be cultivated. Valerian is an excellent plant for unused or waste areas.

Good biennials

Prickly lettuce (*Lactuca serriola*), also called **wild lettuce**, is a winter-growing weed with tall erect stems reaching 60 to 80 centimetres with a much-branched upper section (except in big stands where it can reach 1.5 metres in height). It can grow as an annual or a biennial. It has a slightly spiny stem that produces sticky white sap when broken and a yellow daisy-like flower.

Prickly lettuce is susceptible to hand-pulling but as much of the root should be removed as possible. Use gloves — some people react to the milky latex juice. Prevent prickly lettuce seeding by timely mowing. I certainly encourage it in waste areas. The seed of prickly lettuce has the typical daisy-family wind-catching parachute, like a dandelion.

Queen Anne's lace (*Daucus carota*) looks a lot like carrot, to which it is closely related. It has a large taproot and umbels of white flowers that attract beneficial insects. The root is edible and the flowers look great in a vase. To remove Queen Anne's lace, pull it out by hand or hoe while young. Let it grow under or around fruit trees to lure in predatory wasps that will control codling moth, light brown apple moth and many other pests. Do not confuse with water dropwort (*Oenanthe pimpinelloides*), which is toxic.

Good perennials

Bamboo (*Bambusa* species) is an excellent perennial smother crop. Select non-running bamboos or grow running varieties in a pot. Alternatively, provide a substantial physical barrier between bamboo and sensitive areas, such as 40 to 60 centimetres of galvanized iron buried into the ground. Digging through thick bamboo rhizomes to sever the roots can be very hard work indeed, so it is best to plant only better-behaved species.

Cat's ear (*Hypochaeris radicata*) may also be called **false dandelion**. It has toothed leaves and yellow flowers and is easily mistaken for dandelion and has the same culinary uses, but an inferior taste. Some sources claim it is toxic to stock and humans but it is safe to eat in small quantities that can be easily harvested by hand. It can be distinguished from dandelion because it has more than one flower per stem and a solid stem. Dandelion stems are hollow and carry only one flower per stem. Pull or dig out the taproot or mow to reduce seed production.

Coastal galenia (*Galenia pubescens*) is a perennial prostrate shrub with leaves covered with small hair-like scales. It is an excellent groundcover, especially in exposed or coastal areas, but pulls up easily. It can also handle being mown or cut back with a brush-cutter.

Dandelion (*Taraxacum officinale*) forms rosettes of serrated leaves. There are numerous species but *T. officinale* is the most common. Dandelion greens are a source of iron and vitamin C. They should be eaten raw when young or cooked when older. The root is also edible and is dried and ground to make a beverage that is a coffee substitute. The root and unopened flower buds can also be eaten as a stir-fry vegetable but should be par-boiled first to remove bitter flavours. Dandelion flowers are also edible and can be added to salads to provide colour. The general advice when picking any weed leaves for salad use is to pick young leaves, but it is less well known that the best-tasting leaves come from young plants before the flower stalk has developed. New leaves produced after the flower stalk develops will still retain some bitterness. You can substitute the piquancy of rocket, chicory or endive with dandelion in recipes. The yellow flowers of dandelion are attractive to many beneficial insects.

A strong taproot may be 7 centimetres deep, which helps loosen the soil. The long taproot sustains the plant during winter. It is the reason that dandelion is considered a weed, because it regrows readily from even a portion of the root; it also has a tendency to invade lawns. Dandelion spreads by wind-dispersal and by sticking to humans and animal fur.

Hoe plants before they flower or dig out the entire taproot or pull them by hand. Take as much taproot as possible. Water the area the day before you plan to weed, then use a long, narrow tool, such as a flat screwdriver or dandelion digger, or a trowel. Insert the tool as deeply as you can next to the crown of the

NOT SO BITTER

Most bitter greens such as dandelion can be eaten raw when young. The general advice when picking any weed leaves for salad use is to pick young leaves, but it is less well known that the best-tasting leaves come from young plants before the flower stalk has developed. Older leaves can be blanched to remove the bitter flavour. Simply drop the leaves into boiling water for one minute, then remove. If dandelion leaves need further cooking to soften them, change the water and steam or boil them again.

Dandelion

dandelion and wiggle the tool to loosen the soil around the root. Test to see if it is loose by gently tugging on the plant. If there is little resistance, pull the dandelion out of the soil.

Soils with low levels of calcium and in which organic matter breaks down slowly are havens for dandelions, especially lawns. If you have many dandelions in a lawn, fertilise in the autumn with compost and rock phosphate. The phosphate will improve calcium levels and encourage microbes. Improve competitiveness of grasses by mowing high and leave some clippings on the lawn. Dig existing dandelions before they go to seed. In garden beds mulch will severely restrict the number of dandelions that germinate.

Plantain (*Plantago* species), also known as **ribwort**, is a perennial with a large taproot. It will die readily if the taproot is hoed below ground. It also pulls quite freely in moist soil. Plantain smothers many other weeds, and like many other taproot plants, when they are pulled or chipped a large area of ground underneath

Plantain

is opened up. The taproot loosens soil. The soil fallowed under plantain improves in organic-matter content and friability. Where plantains are dominant, add calcium, compost or compost tea and consider aerating soil to discourage them. Be aware also that there are native plantains that may need protection. Species of native plantain include narrow-leaf plantain (*P. lanceolata*) and broadleafed plantain (*P. major*).

Lawn daisy (*Bellis perennis*) can frustrate some people, but it is actually very attractive and hardy to wetting and drying cycles and mowing. It also flowers for a long time and if it is necessary to cull it back, it is easily pulled from wet soil.

Stinging nettle (*Urtica dioica*) is familiar to many gardeners because of its hairy leaves, which can cause a minor stinging sensation. It is a common weed of fertile soils and often thrives in paddocks around animal camps. It is fast-growing and seeds are long-lived.

Nettles make excellent soup, usually mixed with a starch source such as potatoes or pearl barley.

Nettles have also been long used to make a liquid fertiliser. Nettles produce a great deal of chlorophyll, therefore they are full of iron and micronutrients. The young and actively growing plants produce a lot of nitrogen. Older plants accumulate potassium and

---

Nettle soup

This is a soup I really enjoy. A warning: do not eat raw stinging nettle. Always use gloves when picking nettle.

1. Select only the tips and young leaves of nettle from a hygienic area.
2. Lightly cook an onion in butter or olive oil.
3. Add the nettles; cover and sweat the leaves until limp.
4. Add vegetable or chicken stock to just cover and continue cooking.
5. Pass the cooked nettles through a Mouli food mill to remove some of the fibre. If you don't have a food mill, a blender is fine.
6. Boil the potatoes separately to make a starchy potato stock.
7. Combine the potato stock, nettle and a little of the vegetable or chicken stock.
8. Serve with a little cream or yoghurt and freshly ground pepper or nutmeg.

A food mill is the ideal kitchen utensil for nettle soup as it removes a lot of fibre and produces a much finer-textured soup. Spice lovers can try this recipe with the addition of several pieces of ginger, or several chillies, to the stock. Remove them before blending.

phosphorous. The plants can be simply steeped in water and the resulting liquid diluted to the colour of weak tea. Use as a foliar spray or soil drench. Alternatively, squeeze leaves under heavy bricks, collect the dark liquid that oozes out, and use it as a foliar spray or soil drench. Use young, mature or senescent plants to provide different nutrients, as per the information above.

Violet (*Viola hederacea* or *V. banksii*) are colourful Australian natives that make great groundcovers. *V. banksii* is sometimes grown as an ornamental. *V. hederacea* is a little less showy, but more hardy. Violet flowers are edible.

White clover or **Dutch clover** (*Trifolium repens*) is a creeping legume that provides excellent groundcover, free nitrogen and attracts beneficial insects. It is easily dug with a hand fork when soil is moist and makes excellent compost. Leave the roots with nodules in the soil to benefit garden plants or pull them to enhance compost production. Very high nitrogen levels will discourage clover and some books recommend sulphate of ammonia. Stale urine is a more organic method.

Yarrow (*Achillea millefolium*), also called **milfoil**, is a vigorous spreading weed that can be an excellent groundcover in the right situation. It's good for holding steep banks in place and providing long-lasting colour. It protects and improves soils and makes a great compost ingredient; soil from under a yarrow patch can be added to compost as an activator. It can become very invasive and will need regular attention.

The vigorous growth can overwhelm some gardeners and it spreads quickly from seed and runners.

> Love your weeds: you can eat them, compost them, enjoy their flowers and appreciate their ecological role.

Beware yarrow in locations where it can invade and suppress more desirable plants. Dig it and thoroughly remove running roots and put them in the compost.

5
Environmental weeds

Principle 1: *Always work from areas with native plants towards weed-infested areas.*

Native plants, if given a fair chance, can and will take back the ground that exotic plants have taken from them.

Principle 2: *Make minimal disturbance*
Work with extreme care

Principle 3: *Let native plant regeneration dictate rate of weed removal. The better the condition of the bush, the greater the area that can profitably be weeded at any one time and place.*

Joan Bradley, Bringing Back the Bush (2002),
New Holland, Sydney

WEED INVASION

Invasive species, including weeds, animal pests and diseases, represent the biggest threat to our biodiversity after habitat loss. Weed invasions change the natural diversity and balance of ecological communities. These changes threaten the survival of many plants and animals because the weeds compete with native plants for space, nutrients, pollinators, water and sunlight.

Environmental weeds are any plants that have a negative impact on the natural landscape, most often because they cause a reduction in biodiversity. The eventual impact of species change may result in loss of food sources for wildlife, reduced nesting sites, shelter for feral animals, water pollution from leaves, erosion and subsequently siltation, and an alteration in soil chemistry and changes to moisture regimes that may also influence and change fire intensity and frequency.

Camphor laurel (*Cinnamomum camphora*), blackberry (*Rubus* species), boneseed (*Chrysanthemoides monilifera*), bridal creeper (*Asparagus asparagoides*), watsonia (*Watsonia* species), Cape broom (*Genista monspessulana*), Cape tulip (*Homeria* species), gorse (*Ulex europaeus*), hawthorn (*Crataegus laevigata)*, erica (*Erica* species), fountain grass (*Pennisetum setaceum*), polygala (*Polygala myrtifolia* var. *myrtifolia*), sweet pittosporum, (*Pittosporum* species) and olive (*Olea europaea*) are all examples of environmental weeds in Australia.

Many other weeds described in Chapters 3 and 4 can become environmental weeds if they establish in native bush, grassland or other natural areas.

Each state has a system of proclaiming environmental weeds, but proclaimed plants usually represent only the most common invaders of natural areas. Many environmental weeds are not proclaimed.

Many environmental weed species were originally garden plants and can still be purchased from nurseries. Be aware when buying garden plants that some species can spread into the bush.

GREEN WASTE DISPOSAL

Dumping garden waste in bushland is one of the main ways weeds escape from gardens and start growing in bush or waterways. Some of the ways that you can help minimise the spread of weeds through responsible disposal of garden waste include:

- never dump garden waste over the fence or in bushland
- compost weeds that reproduce vegetatively after drying them on a garden path or shed roof
- cover your compost so that seeds cannot be distributed by wind or animals
- dispose of tougher weeds that reproduce vegetatively by placing them in a black plastic bag, sealing it and 'baking it' in the sun
- be careful when mulching weeds — try to avoid mowing them when they have mature seeds
- remove seed heads from plants before seed has time to mature and disperse
- if taking green waste to a collection point or council green waste tip, transport it carefully and cover trailer loads.

Your local council can tell you about garden waste disposal facilities in your area.

SELECTING GARDEN PLANTS

Garden escapees can become major weeds of native bushlands and threaten native plants and animals. To avoid adding to environmental weed problems follow these simple guidelines:

- learn to identify the weeds in your local area. Local councils may provide a list of common garden escapees. Ask your garden retailer if unsure
- avoid problem plants in your garden. Use safe alternatives, such as sterile forms of species that normally set seed
- use indigenous plants where possible
- do not buy plants from fetes and markets if you don't know what they are

- monitor the garden to ensure that plants are not spreading and threatening bushland or neighbours.

*Remember that even common garden plants such as arum lily (*Zantedeschia aethiopica*), agapanthus (*Agapanthus praecox*) and gazania (*Gazania *species) can become invasive. Do not use waterweeds in ponds — birds can carry them from the pond to local rivers and lagoons.*

GENERAL GARDEN MAINTENANCE

Monitor weedy areas regularly in your garden to check on growth, flowering and seed set.

Plant unused areas with groundcover plants to encourage desirable plants and keep weeds from establishing. Make sure you only buy weed-free soil and mulch. Do not allow fertilisers to run off into bushland — this will encourage weeds also.

The Bradley method

The Bradley method is an important concept to understand if you need to carry out weed control over significant areas of native vegetation. Some of the key principles of the Bradley method apply equally as well to domestic situations.

Two Sydney sisters, Joan and Eileen Bradley, developed the Bradley method during the 1970s. They dedicated thousands of hours to hand control of bushland weeds. They noted the tactics that seemed to work best and developed them into a system that now bears their name.

The Bradley sisters were strictly organic in their work, but since then the method has been adapted to include chemicals, especially the 'cut and swab' method. This adaptation should strictly be called the 'modified Bradley method', to distinguish it from the original, non-chemical approach.

Much more could be said about the Bradley method and anyone spending a lot of time controlling weeds in bushland should consult

Joan Bradley's book, *Bringing Back the Bush* (2002, New Holland, Sydney) and Robin Buchanan's excellent book, *Bush Regeneration* (1996, Open Training and Education Network, Redfern).

The key concepts involved in the Bradley method are outlined here:
- work at a scale that is relevant to the capacity of the indigenous flora to re-establish itself (not too much at one time)
- start with the area of least infestation. This is where native vegetation will have the best chance to re-colonise
- work carefully to disturb the soil as little as possible

Further concepts embodied in the Bradley method are:
- deal with weeds that produce a lot of seed, for example privet (*Ligustrum lucidum*) and pampas grass (*Cortaderia selloana*) as a first priority. This will reduce the capacity of these weeds to re-establish. Also give priority to aggressive vines, climbers and weeds that can produce a very dense canopy, for example lantana (*Lantana* species) and morning glory (*Ipomoea indica*)
- totally remove all plants that can regenerate from a node, for example wandering Jew (*Tradescantia albiflora*)
- only move into a new area as the cleaned-up area regenerates.

These rules have proven themselves over the years. While it is tempting to wade into the blackberries with a brush hook — and a lot can be achieved using this method in a short time — it will most likely grow straight back. By moving slowly and not opening up too big an area, the bush reclaims its own space.

If the bush has been compromised for a long period and seed and propagules of native plants are scarce, bush regenerators will place seed or seedlings of native plants as they work.

Proceed with TLC

- Look around. Know where the native plants are before you start work.
- Choose the most selective weeding technique for the plant and the location.
- Adapt to the season, weather and local conditions. Don't pull or grub weeds when the soil is dry because roots will break off when pulled. Tramping will cause compaction in really wet soil.
- Minimise traffic over the site and wear soft-soled shoes. Do not drag foliage through the bush.
- Wear gloves and personal protective gear.
- Pull the small weeds growing underneath larger woody weeds before you tackle the big ones.
- Avoid damage to native plants as much as possible.
- Disturb the soil as little as possible. Place your thumb and fingers either side of weed seedlings and pull the roots through your hand to hold soil down (use your feet for larger ones).
- Replace any soil disturbed by pulling weeds. Press the soil back down and replace leaf litter over the top.
- Remove from bushland any parts of weeds that could regrow including mature seeds, seed heads with seed that could mature, bulbs, rhizomes and runners. Break up any remaining parts that may be capable of growing into small pieces and leave them on the soil surface as a mulch.
- Follow up your work and finish each area thoroughly before moving on to weed a new patch.
- Work at an appropriate scale for the site and workforce you have available. Don't create large openings.

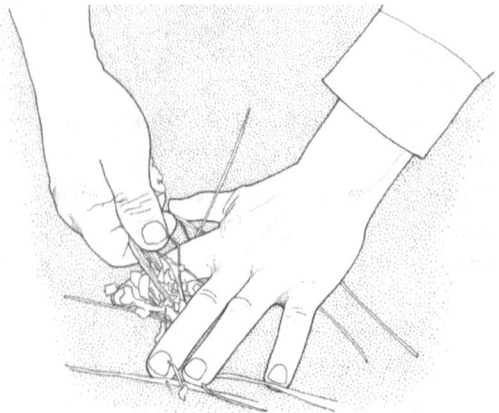
Fingers hold down the soil while the other hand pulls on the weed

Be waterwise

Use special care near creeks and other waterways. These areas are very important habitat for wildlife, and water will move soil and weed propagules that cause harm to downstream areas. Staged removal of weeds along creek lines and in important wildlife sites is often a better strategy than complete removal, which may destroy shelter and nesting sites for small native animals and birds. Start control upstream whenever possible — this will help to limit introduction of new weed seed and revegetate cleared areas to establish some wildlife shelter before moving onto the next section.

LIST OF ENVIRONMENTAL WEEDS

Note: Many of the weeds listed in Chapter 3 can also be considered environmental weeds. This is an indicative list only, designed to illustrate the general methods available for the control of environmental weeds.

African daisy (*Senecio pterophorus*) grows to 3 metres tall in ideal sites. It is easily pulled but all soil should be knocked off the roots or the stems broken up as any formed seed may otherwise mature even after pulling. Break up the stem, or hang pulled plants in the air away from surrounding plants to desiccate the stems and stop seed development. If you cannot get to pull all the weeds, do try to limit seed production by removing developing flowers and seed heads.

Blackberry (*Rubus fruticosus*) is a pernicious weeds of bushland, especially in wet gullies and alongside streams, but also persistent in dry areas and wasteland. Seeds are widely dispersed by birds and they can self-layer from root tips.

Blackberry must be cut down and dug out. My preferred tool is a mattock. The woody crown root of established blackberry plants lift surprisingly easily if the soil is in good condition. Wear gloves and overalls, and sunglasses (to protect your eyes from thorns).

The rust released as a biological control agent initially affected only some of the 23 invasive *Rubus* species. This resulted in a change in the species or variety of blackberry rather than control, but release of a new selection of rusts with the potential for virulence in each of the different types may have more effect.

Blackberry is a Weed of National Significance.

Boneseed or **bitou bush** (*Chrysanthemoides monilifera*) is an upright, woody, evergreen South African shrub, introduced as a garden plant in the late 1800s. It can invade a range of native habitats from sclerophyll forest to coastal heath in all states except Queensland and the Northern Territory. Up to 50,000 seed are produced per plant and they are spread by water or animals.

It can be grubbed or hand-pulled. If working in bushland, learn to identify local natives that might look like boneseed, as the daisy-like flower heads have several native look-alikes.

Boneseed is a Weed of National Significance.

Bridal creeper (*Asparagus asparagoides*) is a climbing herb or vine to 3 metres, arising from a short rhizome attached to tuberous roots. It invades bushland in all states except Queensland and the Northern Territory. Individual plants can produce many seeds, which are dispersed by birds, rabbits and foxes.

Several biological control agents have been released, with the rust fungus *Puccinia myrsiphylli* being the most successful. The bridal creeper leafhopper (*Zyginia* species) has also had some impact. The tubers must be removed by hand-digging. Bridal creeper can be confused with native plants such as old man's beard (*Clematis microphylla*) and *Muehlenbeckia* species.

Bridal creeper is a Weed of National Significance.

Cape broom (*Genista monspessulana*) can be grubbed or pulled. Use a tree-popper for large shrubs. Large roots must be removed from the soil and repeated hand-pulling of seedlings will be required for many years. Long-lived broom seed in the soil can be encouraged by smoking. I removed a quarter of an acre of tall dense broom infestation from the Stirling property and was facing many years of repeated weed control. Instead, I created many very small fires, burning the remains of the broom plants and some additional twiggy material shed by our many gums. Where fire is intense, seed at or near the soil surface is destroyed, but surrounding seed is triggered to germinate by chemicals in the smoke. Several weeks later I found neat rings of germinated broom seedlings, which I then pulled. This removed the problem in two years rather than 10.

English broom (*Cytisus scoparius*) is a leguminous shrub growing 2 to 3 metres in height, with a yellow pea flower. It produces a hard-coated seed that can be long-lived in the soil. Pull small plants or grub larger ones. Use a tree-popper to remove the whole plant or cut stems right to the soil surface (higher than 2 centimetres and they will re-grow). Seedling regrowth will need to be pulled, possibly for several years. Flaming works very well while the young plant still has its dicotyledonous leaves. Seed near the soil surface can be 'smoked' to stimulate germination, using small fires or a smoke gun similar to a beekeeper's tool.

Broom can be used as a brush-fencing material.

Erica (*Erica* species) is a serious bushland invader in high rainfall areas. It is not susceptible to chemical controls; however, it exhibits a physical weakness that makes it a good target for a physical control method called 'sway and snap'. The crown root area becomes swollen into a small lignotuber (woody tuber) like a mallee tree. The junction of the lignotuber and the roots underneath is brittle and subject to breaking. Grab plants and sway them back and forth to weaken this fragile spot. It will eventually come away leaving the taproot behind (only the lignotuber can re-grow). For stubborn plants, whack the side of the lignotuber hard with a small sledgehammer while pulling on the top with the other hand. Remove multi-branched tops with a saw to gain access to the lignotuber. With smaller lignotubers, a strong kick with a work boot may substitute for the sledgehammer.

Gorse (*Ulex europaeus*), also known as **furze** or **furse**, is a serious invasive weed of bushland and roadsides. Gorse can be grubbed but it is thorny and unpleasant to work with, and so is often controlled by flail mowing or burning. Larger populations are bulldozed and burnt. Young seedlings and regrowth are much more easily controlled than the established mature bushes. Seedlings will require attention for several years after controlling larger plants.

Gorse flowers are edible in salads and are used to make a herbal tea and a 'wine'. Sheep and goats will graze gorse, especially young plants that have not become very thorny. High stocking rates are required for this to be an effective control method. Several biological control agents are available for gorse, including gorse seed weevil (*Exapion ulicis*), gorse thrips (*Sericothrips staphylinus*) and gorse spider mite (*Tetranychus lintearius*), but they are not very effective.

Gorse is a Weed of National Significance.

Lantana (*Lantana camara*) is a reasonably harmless garden plant in southern Australia but a serious bushland invader in high rainfall areas on the east coast. It spreads by seeds and layering.

Layering allows lantana to form very dense stands and therefore harbour vermin. Foxes and birds pass the seed in their droppings. Germination rate of seed is generally low unless it has been through the gut of an animal. Lantana releases allelopathic chemicals into the soil to prevent germination of some other plant species. Lantana is also toxic to stock.

Release biological controls and tackle small infestations by grubbing. Use mechanical methods and fire to tame larger infestations and revegetate affected areas. Various biological control agents have been released with mixed results. Some agents are specific to varieties of lantana.

Lantana is a Weed of National Significance.

Mimosa (*Mimosa pigra*) is a prickly invasive shrub that makes dense thickets throughout tropical and subtropical regions. A number of biological control agents have been released, including a stem-boring moth, a beetle that eats the seeds, and a weevil.

Mimosa is a Weed of National Significance.

Watsonia (*Watsonia* species) is slow to establish but develops very dense and long-lasting populations. It grows from a flattened corm encased in a tunic of coarse fibres. The root system, while quite shallow, is also dense and fibrous. Watsonia produces a fan-shaped cluster of five to seven erect, sword-shaped leaves up to 1 metre long that grow directly from the underground corm. Flowering stems appear in spring, growing 1.5 to 2 metres tall and turning red as they mature. Watsonia does not reproduce by seeds but grows clusters of bulbils (more correctly cormils) on the stem just below the flowers.

Ornamental watsonia varieties are available from nurseries and while these species should not become established as weeds, people living close to bushland should use care.

The shallow root system is the key to removal of watsonia. The corm must be removed completely, which is best done with a mattock or a tool such as the twork (see page 103). Stop development

Watsonia

of the cormils by mowing or cutting flower stalks with secateurs. Bag the stems with cormils attached and burn or dispose of them in the hard rubbish. The mature corms are also very difficult to destroy. Small quantities should be broken into small pieces and composted. Larger quantities should be placed in hard rubbish or burned. The fibrous tunic covering the corm is very resistant to composting, fermenting or shredding. I have kept watsonia corms under water with seaweed extract, humates and other added products for 12 months and they still did not ferment.

For larger infestations mow or brush-cut watsonia after the flowers are produced and it will not send up another tall flower spike. It may regrow leaves, which can be used to identify the location of the corm for further control activities.

Weeds of waterways

Cabomba (*Cabomba caroliniana*) is a submerged freshwater plant originally introduced for use in aquariums. Plants are usually rooted in soil, but stem fragments may float on the water surface. Populations can become very dense and completely clog waterways with their long stems. Small areas may be pulled by hand, but in deep water that method requires scuba gear.

Cabomba is a Weed of National Significance.

Salvinia (*Salvinia molesta*) is a serious invasive aquatic weed. It is a fern that floats on still or slow-moving water and destroys the habitat for fish or other animals. Because it makes such dense populations, quarantine is critical to limit its spread. It is almost impossible to eradicate once established. It can grow rapidly to cover the entire water surface of still or slow-moving water bodies forming a thick mat of free-floating vegetation, especially if nutrient levels, are high. It excludes light and reduces oxygen levels, causing problems for birds, fish and invertebrates. Salvinia slows water flow, limits stock access and improves conditions for mosquitoes to breed. It blocks pumps and stops boats.

Salvinia is native to southeastern Brazil. It was introduced to Australia for use in aquaria and ponds.

Salvinia is a Weed of National Significance.

Water hyacinth (*Eichhornia crassipes*) is a serious aquatic perennial weed which forms a floating mat that spreads from stolons and seed. It thrives in high-nutrient water. Dense mats of vegetation reduce oxygen and light for other aquatic organisms and restrict navigation, fishing and recreation. It is almost impossible to eradicate once established.

6
Weed control quick reference

Use this chapter as a quick reference guide to take action against common weeds in your garden, on your property or around your general environment. The information on these pages sets out ways to deal with various weed species. It is not possible to list every plant considered as a weed, but weeds with similar characteristics are very likely susceptible to the same control measures. If you have a weed not listed in this chapter, find those with a similar growth form or habit and apply the controls suggested in the table.

Common/scientific name	Hand pull	Dig	Mulch	Smother crop
African daisy (*Senecio pterophorus*)	Yes	Hoe or dig	Yes	Yes
African lovegrass (*Eragrostis curvula*)	Not effective	Mechanical hoeing spreads this grass	Not effective	After other control methods
Artichoke thistle (*Cynara cardunculus*)	Yes	Yes	After other control methods	After other control methods
Barleygrass (*Hordeum glaucum*)	Not effective	For small areas	Yes	Yes
Bathurst burr (*Xanthium spinosum*)	Too thorny	Hoe	After hoeing	Must be very competitive
Blackberry (*Rubus fruticosus*)	No except when very small	Yes — slash first	After other controls	Yes
Blackberry nightshade (*Solanum nigrum*)	Yes	Hoe when small	Yes	For young seedlings
Bindii or jo-jo (*Soliva sessilis*)	When very small	Hoe when small	After other controls	Yes
Boneseed (*Chrysanthemoides monilifera*)	• Pull when small • Use tree-popper on larger plants	Hoe when small	After other controls	Not very effective
Bracken fern (*Pteridium esculentum*)	Not very effective	Grub or fork and remove underground parts	After other controls	Not very effective

Weed control quick reference

Biological	Thermal	Organic herbicide	Cultural controls and notes
No	Not very effective	While small	• Stop seed production • Break up pulled stems to prevent seed set
No	Needs repeated application	Not effective	• Prevent introduction and spread as first priority
No	While small	While small	• Slash or graze with goats or sheep
No	While small		• Graze
Fungus in moist areas only	While small	While small	• Annual, so prevent seed production • Germinates over a long seasonal period, so revisit from time to time to control new volunteers
Yes, but not very effective	Burning may be part of the control program	For young seedlings	• Graze with goats
No	For seedlings	For seedlings	• Stop seed production
No	• Flame young seedlings. • Rake and burn seed	Yes	• Stop seed production • Collect and remove seed
Various insects, mites and fungi under investigation	Fire will stimulate seeds to germinate all at once	No	• Stop seed production • Some native plants look similar to boneseed
No	Repeated flaming will slow growth	No	• Mow repeatedly to weaken growth

Common/scientific name	Hand pull	Dig	Mulch	Smother crop
Buttercup (*Ranunculus repens*)	Easily pulled but some people are sensitive to skin irritation from buttercup so gloves are recommended	Can be hoed easily	Mulch will restrict germination	Must be strongly competitive
Caltrop (*Tribulus terrestris*)	When small	Yes, but unpleasant once seed is produced	After other controls	Yes
Cape broom (*Genista monspessulana*)	When small	Grub with a mattock or use a tree-popper	After other controls	After other controls
Capeweed (*Arctotheca calendula*)	When young	Yes	Yes	Yes
Cat's ear (*Hypochaeris radicata*)	Yes	Yes	Yes	Yes
Chickweed (*Stellaria media*)	Yes	Yes	Yes	Yes
Chicory (*Cichorium* species)	Yes	Yes	Yes	Yes
Cleavers or goosegrass (*Galium aparine*)	Yes	Yes	Yes	Yes
Cabomba (*Cabomba caroliniana*)	Yes, if you can access the roots under water	With an excavator, but expensive and a high risk of rapid regrowth	No	No

Weed control quick reference

Biological	Thermal	Organic herbicide	Cultural controls and notes
No	Effective for small seedlings	Yes	• Easily controlled while small but large plants have a surprisingly strong grip on the ground
No	• Flame young seedlings • Rake and burn seed	Yes	• Stop seed production • Remove seed
Under investigation	• Burning may be part of the control program • Flame regrowth seedlings	No	• Cut stems at ground level
Yes	When young	When young	• Graze • Will harbour red-legged earth mite
No	Yes	Yes	• Graze
No	Yes	Yes	• Graze with poultry • Will harbour red-legged earth mite and whitefly
No	Yes	Yes	• Graze
No	Yes	Yes	• Graze
No	No	No	• Quarantine and early response to invasion is very important to prevent establishment

Common/scientific name	Hand pull	Dig	Mulch	Smother crop
Couch grass (*Agropyron repens*)	No	• With a fork • Remove all underground parts	No	No
Creeping bent grass (*Agrostis stolonifera*)	No	• With a fork • Remove all underground parts	No	No
Cress (*Cardamine hirsuta*)	Yes	Yes	Yes	Yes
Dandelion (*Taraxacum officinale*)	When young	Yes	Yes	Yes
Dock (*Rumex* species)	When young	Yes	Yes	Yes
English broom (*Cytisus scoparius*)	• When young • Use tree-popper when older	Yes	Yes	After other controls
Feather grass or feather top (*Pennisetum villosum*)	No	For small areas	After other controls	After other controls
Fat hen (*Chenopodium album*)	Yes	Yes	Yes	Yes
Fleabane (*Conyza* and *Erigeron* species)	Yes	Hoe when small	Yes	Yes
Forget-me-not (*Myosotis arvensis*)	Yes, before seed set	Yes, before seed set	Yes	Yes
Fumitory (*Fumaria* species)	Yes, before seed set	Yes, before seed set	Yes	Yes

Weed control quick reference

Biological	Thermal	Organic herbicide	Cultural controls and notes
No	Temporary control only		• Use black plastic method or solarisation • Pulled material may regrow • Dry it out before composting or put it in a plastic bag and allow it to ferment, then compost
No	Temporary control only		• Pulled material may regrow • Use black plastic method or solarisation
No	Yes	Yes	• Edible leaves
No	Yes	Yes	• Edible leaves and root
No	When young	Yes	• Graze when young
No	Burning may be part of a control strategy	No	• Prevent from setting seed
No	Yes, graze or mow first to reduce tops and expose growing point	Yes	• Difficult to control so prevent establishment and control spread as a first priority
No	When young	When young	• Prevent from setting seed
No	When small	• When small • Mow first if plants are tall and spray regrowth	• As seed is short-lived (2–3 years) prevent seed production
No	Yes	Yes	• Makes an attractive cover crop in waste areas
No	Yes	Yes	• Rambles over plants and structures but pulls easily

Common/scientific name	Hand pull	Dig	Mulch	Smother crop
Gorse or furse (*Ulex europaeus*)	• When small • When large, use a tree-popper	Grub with a mattock	After other treatment	After other treatment
Green amaranth (*Amaranthus viridis*)	When small	Yes	Yes	Yes
Groundsel (*Senecio* species)	• Yes • Use tree-popper for large bushes	Yes	After other controls	After other controls
Guildford grass (*Romulea rosea*)	When soil is moist	When soil is moist	After other controls	Yes
Horehound (*Marrubium vulgare*)	When soil is moist	Hoe	After other controls	After other controls
Johnson grass (*Sorghum halepense*)	No	• For small areas • Remove all fleshy roots	After other controls	After other controls
Mallow (*Malvia* species)	When small	Hoe	Yes	Yes
Morning glory (*Ipomoea indica*)	No	Yes, remove all large roots	No	No
Lantana (*Lantana camara*)	When small cut taller plants, work stump back and forth to loosen soil, then pull	Cut or slash first, then dig roots	After other controls	After other controls

Weed control quick reference

Biological	Thermal	Organic herbicide	Cultural controls and notes
Yes, but not very effective	• Burning may be part of the control program • Young seedlings can be flamed	For young seedlings	• Chain or push large infestations • Cut to ground level • Will require follow-up control of seedlings
No	When small	When small	• Can become a useful smother crop but needs watching to control its spread
Many insects have been introduced. Several moths and beetles and a fly are effective, depending on the region. Get advice from a local professional	When small	When small	• Aerate soil • Add compost and compost tea
No	No	No	• Aerate and loosen soil • Add gypsum
No	Burning may be part of a control program, especially to remove seed	When small	• Use horehound tea to protect against colds
No	No	Slash first to expose growing point	• Crimp in late spring • Very aggressive grass so avoid introducing if possible
No	When small	When small	• Seed of mallow is edible
No	No	No	• Must remove all lateral roots
Various biological control agents released with mixed results	Burning may be part of a control program	No	• Will require follow-up visits

Common/scientific name	Hand pull	Dig	Mulch	Smother crop
Lawn daisy (*Bellis perennis*)	When soil is moist	Yes	After other controls	After other controls
Noogoora burr (*Xanthium occidentale*)	When soil is moist and burr is young	Digging is effective on small infestations	After other controls	After other controls
Nut grass (*Cyperus rotundus*)	No	Yes	After other controls	After other controls
Onion weed (*Asphodelus fistulosus*)	No	Yes, but requires some effort	After other controls	After other controls
Pampas grass (*Cortaderia selloana*)	No	Yes. Use a bobcat or excavator for large plants	After other controls	After other controls
Paspalum (*Paspalum dilatatum*)	When small	When soil is moist	After other controls	After other controls
Paterson's curse or salvation Jane (*Echium plantagineum*)	When soil is moist	Yes	After other controls	After other controls
Pearlwort (*Sagina procumbens*)	Yes	Yes, but pulling is adequate because it will not regrow from roots	After other controls	Yes
Pennyroyal (*Mentha pulegium*)	When small	Yes	After other controls	After other controls
Periwinkle (*Vinca major*) and lesser periwinkle (*Vinca minor*)	Roots are very brittle; loosen soil first with a fork, then pull roots	• Yes • Remove as much root as possible	No	After other controls

Weed control quick reference

Biological	Thermal	Organic herbicide	Cultural controls and notes
No	Not very effective	No	• Digging is effective
• Several beetles and a fly released with poor results • Rust disease *Puccinia xanthii* established in some areas	When small	When small	• Prevent seed production
No	To reduce vigour	No	• Aerate soil
No	No	No	• Avoid introduction if possible
No	Burning may be part of the control program, especially to remove the crown roots after cutting the tops down	No	• Avoid introduction if possible
No	When small	When small	• Graze • Avoid introduction if possible
Yes	When small	When small	• Graze
No	Yes	Yes	• Control before seed set
No	When small	When small	• Has some culinary uses
No	No	No	• Will require follow-up visits

Common/scientific name	Hand pull	Dig	Mulch	Smother crop
Petty spurge (*Euphorbia peplus*)	• Yes • Use gloves	Yes	Yes	Yes
Plantain (*Plantago* species)	When soil is moist	Yes	Yes	Yes
Purslane (*Portulaca oleracea*)	When soil is moist	Yes	Yes	Yes
Prickly lettuce (*Lactuca serriola*)	When soil is moist	Yes	Yes	Yes
Prickly pear (*Opuntia* species)	No	Yes	No	After other controls
Privet (*Ligustrum lucidum*)	When small	• Yes • Use tree-popper for larger bushes	After other controls	After other controls
Ragwort (*Senecio jacobaea*)	Yes	Yes	After other controls	After other controls
Ryegrass (*Lolium* species)	Yes	Hoe small plants and fork larger ones	Yes	After other controls
Saffron thistle (*Carthamus lanatus*)	Use gloves	Hoe small plants and fork or mattock larger ones	After other controls	Yes
Scarlet pimpernel (*Anagallis arvensis*)	Yes	Hoe	Yes	Yes
Shepherd's purse (*Capsella bursa-pastoris*)	Yes	Hoe	Yes	Yes
Silver-leaf nightshade (*Solanum elaeagnifolium*)	Yes	Hoe	Yes	Yes

Weed control quick reference

Biological	Thermal	Organic herbicide	Cultural controls and notes
No	No	Yes	• Use gloves as latex sap may cause irritation • Use eye protection for larger spurge species
No	When small	Yes	• Can host some sucking pests so clear away from sensitive plants if pests appear
No	Yes	Yes	• All parts are edible
No	When small	Yes	• Use gloves as sap may cause irritation
Yes	• No • Dry then burn old plants to destroy	No	• Use gloves and eye protection
No	When small	When small	• Look for seedlings under bird roosts
Various insect controls available	When small	When small	• Aerate soil • Add compost and compost tea
No	When small	Mow first	• Graze
No	When small	Mow first	• Graze
No	Yes	Yes	• Easy to pull by hand
No	Yes	Yes	• Easy to pull by hand
No	Yes	Yes	• Easy to pull by hand when small

Common/scientific name	Hand pull	Dig	Mulch	Smother crop
Skeleton weed (*Chondrilla juncea*)	When soil is moist	Yes	After other controls	Yes
Sorrel (*Rumex acetosella*)	When soil is moist	Trace lateral roots and remove	No	After other controls
Soursob (*Oxalis pes-caprae*)	When soil is moist but some bulbs will be left behind	Use care to remove as many bulbs as possible	No	No
Sow thistle (*Sonchus oleraceus*)	Young plants in moist soil	Yes	Yes	Yes
St John's wort (*Hypericum perforatum*)	Young plants in moist soil	Yes	After other controls	Yes
Stinging nettle — perennial (*Urtica dioica*)	• Young plants • Use gloves	Hoe	Yes	Yes
Stinging nettle — annual (*Urtica urens*)	• Young plants • Use gloves	Hoe	Yes	Yes
Summer grass (*Digitaria sanguinalis*)	When soil is moist	Remove all the spreading stems	After other controls	After other controls
Sweet pittosporum (*Pittosporum undulatum*)	When small	Grub in the spring	No	No
Three-cornered garlic (*Allium triquetrum*)	When soil is moist	Yes	Ineffective	Ineffective
Turnip weed (*Rapistrum rugosum*)	When small	Yes	Yes	Yes

Weed control quick reference

Biological	Thermal	Organic herbicide	Cultural controls and notes
Yes	• When small • Burn to remove seed	Use a lower dose of organic herbicide to prevent seed from setting	• Prevent from seeding if possible
No	No	No	• Remove as much root as possible
No	No	Repeated applications	• Will need repeat visits
No	When small	Slash first if growth is tall	• All parts are edible
No	• When small • Burn to remove seed	Slash first if growth is tall	• Graze with goats or sheep but not when St John's wort is flowering • Stop seed production
No	When small	When small	• Edible leaves
No	When small	When small	• Edible leaves
No	Temporary control	May need repeated treatments	• Control before seed set
No	No	No	• Cut close to the ground or ringbark the stem • Prevent seed production
No	• When small • Will need repeated treatment	No	• Mow to control bulbil production
No	When small	When small	• Prevent seed production

WEED

Common/scientific name	Hand pull	Dig	Mulch	Smother crop
Valerian (*Valeriana officinalis*)	When small	Yes	Yes	Yes
Variegated thistle (*Silybum marianum*)	When small	Yes	Yes	Yes
Wandering Jew (*Tradescantia albiflora*)	No	Yes	Ineffective	Not very effective
Water hyacinth (*Eichhornia crassipes*)	• Yes • Remove all vegetative material because regrowth can be rapid	Not applicable	No	No
Winter grass (*Poa annua*)	Yes	Yes	Yes	Yes
Wild oats (*Avena* species)	In small areas	In small areas	Yes	Yes
Wild radish (*Raphanus raphanistrum*)	In small areas	In small areas	Yes	Yes
Wireweed (*Polygonum aviculare*)	In small areas	Yes	Yes	Yes
Yarrow (*Achillea millefolium*)	No	• Yes • Remove all underground parts	No	Shading from trees may help

Weed control quick reference

Biological	Thermal	Organic herbicide	Cultural controls and notes
No	When small	When small	• Valerian produces attractive flowers and can be tolerated or even encouraged in used parts of the garden
Weevil	When small	When small	• Toxic to sheep and cattle
No	No	No	• Very brittle • Get as much root as possible
Yes	No	No	• Reduce nutrient input to waterway
No	Slash first if tall	Slash first if tall	• Mow or graze to stop seed production
No	Slash first	Slash first if tall	• Graze
No	When small	Slash first if tall	• Avoid soil disturbance to limit germination
No	No	Slash first if tall	• Graze
No	No	No	• Remove all underground parts

7

Glossary and resources

GLOSSARY

Adventitious roots: Roots that arise from an unusual anatomical area of the plant, such as from the stems, leaves or old woody roots.

Acid: Having a pH reaction of less than the neutral level of 7.

Agroecology: The study of ecology in agricultural fields.

Alkaline: Having a pH reaction of more than the neutral level of 7.

Allelopathy: The release of chemical compounds into soil or air by one plant for the purpose of affecting another plant or animals living on the plant. It often involves harmful effects, such as suppression of germination in other plants or the inhibition of growth.

Anaerobic: Occurring in the absence of oxygen.

Biological control: Any living thing or biologically derived substance that controls or reduces the number of pests or weeds.

Bulbil: Small bulb produced above the ground, usually at the junction of stem and leaf. May also be called an 'offset'.

Bulb: Thickened, rounded fleshy bud that stores starch to enable a plant to survive dormant periods. Usually underground. Bulbs have layers of 'scales' that are actually modified leaves (for example, an onion).

Corm: Short, vertical, swollen underground stem that stores starch for use during dormant periods (usually winter but sometimes summer). Corms can produce adventitious roots, leaves and flowers in the following spring or autumn. The outer layer is covered with papery leaves called tunic leaves that protect the corm from water loss or insect attack. Corms can be distinguished from bulbs by the lack of fleshy scales. Watsonia and crocus grow from corms.

Cormil: Small corm, usually produced on aerial stems.

Crucifer: A plant with four flower petals arranged in a cross. Refers to the mustard family (*Cruciferae* or *Brassicaceae*), which includes alyssum, mustard, cabbage, radish, broccoli, and many weed species. May also be called brassicas.

Cultivar: A variety or selection of plant cultivated by selective breeding to preserve certain desirable characteristics.

Dicot: Abbreviation of dicotyledon. A flowering, broadleaf plant that has two seed leaves (cotyledons) when the seed germinates.

Epidermis: The outer (surface) layer of a plant or animal.

Green manure: Plants grown for the purpose of slashing down as mulch or incorporating into the soil.

Groundcover: Low growing plant used to provide weed-resistant full-canopy cover. Selected for their hardiness and ease of cultivation.

Herbicide: A substance that kills weeds or other plants.

Indigenous: Local to a particular biological or geographical area.

Lime: Calcium carbonate. Supplies calcium to soil and affects pH. Neutralises acidic conditions.

Monocot: Abbreviation of monocotyledon. A flowering plant, including grasses, that has only one seed leaf (cotyledon) when the seed germinates.

Parasitoid: A parasite that eventually kills or consumes its host.

pH: Degree of acidity or alkalinity measured on a scale from 0–14, where 7 is neutral.

Propagule: Any structure capable of being propagated or acting as an agent of reproduction. Usually vegetative portions of a plant, such as a bud or other offshoot, that aid in dispersal of the species and from which a new individual may develop.

Rhizome: Horizontal underground stem capable of giving rise to new plants. Rhizomes are the main stem of the plant, whereas stolons arise from the main stem. Occasionally rhizomes may be found at or just above the soil surface, for example iris (*Iris* species).

Rhizosphere: The small zone of soil around a root that is directly influenced by root secretions and associated soil microorganisms.

Roguing: Removing the seed heads of weeds.

Rosette: An array of leaves laying flat against the ground produced from a single stem of a broadleaf biennial or perennial in its first year (or each year) before it produces a seed stalk.

Ruderal: A plant that grows in rubbish heaps, poor soil or wasteland.

Stamen: The male organ of a flower containing the anther, where pollen is produced.

Stolon: Modified horizontal stem that grows at or just below the soil surface. Stolons give rise to new plants from adventitious roots that grow at the ends of the stolon or at nodes. They are often called runners.

Species: The fundamental unit of biological classification, defined as a group of organisms similar in structure and physiology that are capable of producing fertile offspring when mated. Abbreviated to sp. for one species and spp. for more than one species.

Spray grazing: Treating pasture with a low-dose of herbicide prevention to sweeten non-palatable weeds and make them more attractive to stock.

Tuber: Underground starch storage organ that arises by the thickening of a stolon or rhizome; for example, a potato is a tuber or modified stolon.

Vernalised: Exposure of seeds or other plant parts to low temperature for enough time to instigate plant development such as flowering.

RECOMMENDED READING
Weed identification
Hussey, B. M. J., Keighery, G. J., Cousens, R. D., Dodd, J. and Lloyd, S.G. 2007, *Western Weeds: A Guide to the Weeds of Western Australia,* 2nd edn. Weed Society of WA, Victoria Park.

Lamp, Charles and Collet, Frank 1976, *A Field Guide to Weeds in Australia,* Inkata Press, Melbourne.

Parsons and Cuthbertson 1992, *Noxious Plants of Australia,* Inkata Press, Melbourne.

Organic weed control books
Cocannouer, Joseph A. 1950, *Weeds: Guardians of the Soil,* Devon-Adair, Old Greenwich, Connecticut.

French, Jackie 2006, *Organic Control of Common Weeds,* Aird Books, Flemington.

Morgan, Wendy 1990, *Growing Plants Without Herbicides: Chemical-Free Control of Unwanted Plants,* Department of Agriculture and Rural Affairs, Melbourne.

Pfeiffer, Ehrenphried 1981 *Weeds and What They Tell,* Biodynamic Farming and Gardening Association, Oregon.

Walters, Charles 1991, *Weeds: Control Without Poisons,* Acres, Austin, Texas.

Weed control in bushland
Bradley, Joan 2002, *Bringing Back the Bush,* New Holland, Sydney.

Buchanan, Robin A. 1996, *Bush Regeneration: Recovering Australian Landscapes,* Open Training and Education Network, Redfern.

USEFUL WEBSITES
Weed legislation and government weed control strategies

Federal
Quarantine Act 1908 www.daff.gov.au/aqis/quarantine/legislation/quarantine

Biological Control Act 1985 www.austlii.edu.au/au/legis/cth/consol_act/bca1984186

Environment Protection and Biodiversity Conservation Act 1999 www.environment.gov.au/epbc/index.html

Role of states
All states: www.weeds.gov.au/government/roles/state.html

Tasmania
www.dpiw.tas.gov.au/inter.nsf/ThemeNodes/TPRY-52J59L?open

Victoria
Victoria Government www.dpi.vic.gov.au/DPI/nrenfa.nsf/LinkView/05E31F1D1DA3FF59CA256EDF0080F565AD1311E486E564954A2567D80009DE05

Weed Society of Victoria: www.wsvic.org.au

New South Wales
NSW Government: www.dpi.nsw.gov.au/agriculture/pests-weeds/weeds/legislation

Weed Management Society of NSW: nswweedsoc.org.au

Queensland
www.dpi.qld.gov.au/cps/rde/dpi/hs.xsl/4790_8331_ENA_HTML.htm

Northern Territory
www.nt.gov.au/nreta/natres/weeds/index.html

Western Australia
www.agric.wa.gov.au/objtwr/imported_assets/content/pw/weed/bull4490.pdf

The Weeds Society of WA: members.iinet.net.au/~weeds/index.htm

South Australia
SA Government: www.dwlbc.sa.gov.au

Weed Management Society of SA: www.wmssa.org.au/weeds.htm

General weed information
Weeds in Australia — the official Australian web resource on Government weeds, including legislation, identification and control: www.weeds.gov.au

Western Australian weeds: florabase.calm.wa.gov.au/weeds

Tools and seeds
diggers.com.au

Excellent online shop selling hardy plant cultivars and old varieties, books and organic pest control products.

greenharvest.com.au

Excellent online shop selling organic pest control books and products including non-drying glue, floating row covers and insect traps.

General organic information

www.ofa.org.au

Many articles and links about organic growing, standards and regulation, the growth of organic farming and information on pesticides and genetically modified organisms.

www.organicliving.com.au

Australian website about organic food, gardening and lifestyle with many contributions from author Tim Marshall.

www.tmorganics.com

Tim's Marshall's own website, with many bug and weed stories, a blog and a forum.

www.nasaa.com.au

Download the NASAA organic standard from this site. Also has some general articles on organic growing.

www.bfa.com.au

Download the ACO organic standard from this site. Also has many interesting stories and links.

Case study: Tim's garden

I help to maintain several gardens, including property belonging to family members and friends scattered through the central Mount Lofty Ranges in South Australia. I have productive food gardens at several of these locations. The principal garden is at Stirling.

The Stirling garden

The main Stirling garden is 0.4 hectares, running downhill from the crest of a hill and south facing. It had once been a grand Stirling garden, but by the time I arrived some of the old stringybark, pines and deciduous trees had become senescent and overgrown. Friends had lived here for many years and one had been a keen gardener, but in later years he became unwell and unable to keep up the work. It was seriously overgrown with many weed species. About one quarter was taken up by English broom and almost another quarter by blackberries. Dotted everywhere were hawthorn and plum, the occasional cotoneaster, pine, olive and some large *Erica* bushes. An old cork elm was suckering wildly in the front yard and the old hebe hedge had grown lanky and fallen over, grown again and fallen over, and was growing again. Ivy grew up some of the old trees, some patches of watsonia were beginning to establish and a spreading iris had taken over large areas. Three-corner garlic, with Guildford grass growing underneath, was over half the property and there were large patches of *Tradescantia* and soursob, as well as some weedy lilies and a nasty spreading gladiolus. In some areas many of these weeds grew together in a tangled mess. It had a charm of its own and the children who grew up there thought the garden had a magical quality. But large parts of the garden were inaccessible and harboured foxes, rabbits, feral cats and a large population of blackbirds.

The first job was to clear enough blackberry to be able to move around the property to investigate what remained of the old garden. This was accomplished using a large power slasher, a petrol brush-cutter, brush hooks, a sturdy lawnmower and hours of work with secateurs, cutting and carting away blackberry canes. Blackberry roots were grubbed with a mattock. Some blackberry canes were burnt and some were composted or mulched. A small patch of blackberry was left for fruit but this has been gradually reduced as the raspberry patch grows in output.

The next job was to chainsaw some very large, fallen stringybark, all with foxholes or a rabbit warren in their tangled roots. The broom was also a high priority, because although it was restricted to my garden, it threatened to invade neighbouring properties. It was pulled by hand or with a tree-popper, or grubbed with a mattock. Tops were composted, large stems cut for firewood and the remainder was dried, mixed with fallen gum branches and burnt in many small bonfires. The shifting fires burnt some broom seed and smoked the rest to break the dormancy of seed and bring on the germination of as much broom as possible in the next two seasons.

Guildford grass, lilies and oxalis are ongoing projects but significant areas have been cleared. Initially, the underground parts were put into the hard rubbish but I soon decided that there was far too much biomass tied up in these plants and I learnt to compost them thoroughly as follows. The large roots of the lilies are broken up and mixed with oxalis and three-cornered garlic. They are then placed inside a structure made from small, tightly packed hay bales, so the weeds cannot grow through the sides. These difficult-to-compost weeds are collected over at least six months, during which time the older parts of the pile have started to compost nicely. I add very little extra material but I do add an occasional layer of pulverised chicken manure and sometimes fresh horse manure. Non-weed materials make up only about 5 per cent of the pile. Eventually, several very large sheets of cardboard, courtesy of my local whitegoods retailer, are spread over the top of the bales and another compost heap is constructed over the top, using clean ingredients. The entire heap is then left undisturbed for about six to eight months, at which point compost worms are added. Any sign of the weeds has disappeared when the heap is opened up about four months later.

When the major weeds were cleared from an area, another set of annual and perennial weeds became established. They had been around, struggling under blackberry bushes, and they quickly colonised the opened patches. These weeds included chickweed, dandelion, ribwort, prickly lettuce, sow thistle, fumitory, cleavers, white clover and about ten grasses. I am less keen on the grasses, although I am a little more tolerant of the three or four native species, but the entire set of broadleaf weeds are easy for me to manage, so I choose to work with them, allowing them to colonise new ground, selectively weeding around them or thinning them as needed. I like them because they protect and improve the soil underneath — especially the clover and the tap-rooted weeds — they make excellent compost, and they are easy to pull, dig, mow or brush-cut.

When new trees, shrubs or vines are planted they are mulched and often the area will be planted with cover crops or groundcovers comprising a range of drought-tolerant ornamentals and sometimes just the weeds. Groundcovers from weeds often establish from volunteer plants or I may encourage them by simply scattering seed heads (sow thistle) or introducing runners (clover).

Small patches of salvation Jane were completely eliminated within a couple of seasons by digging or pulling the entire root. Blackberry nightshade and African daisy are pulled up on sight and not permitted to produce seed.

Forget-me-not, valerian, various bulbs and hollyhock are also distributed through part of the garden and they are allowed to survive, although I carefully monitor the forget-me-not because it would become dominant. I like the dramatic effect of hollyhock (*Alcea* spp.) arising at random through the garden and have introduced *Delphinium*, stock (*Matthiola incana*) and mullein (*Verbascum thapsus*) to naturalise throughout for the same reason. *Anemone*, *campanula*, *pelargonium* and *coreopsis* have also been introduced at many places. Like any gardener, I have also collected a wide range of other plants but the key species mentioned have been encouraged to naturalise through the garden.

Because I apply lots of compost and mulch, weeds come away easily through most of the year. The most difficult situations occur where there are tree roots near the soil surface.

I travel widely with my work and keep busy, but gardening is both relaxation for me and precious 'thinking time' and I often emerge from the garden with a headful of ideas for non-gardening projects. Because of the travel commitment, I sometimes fall well behind in the planned work schedule, and have to pinch time from wherever possible to catch up. It is not unusual to see me take advantage of a full moon or use my headlamp to extend the gardening hours well past daylight.

Despite having cleared the bulk of the property of a variety of aggressive weeds, chemicals have only been used in two roles. One 15-litre tank of roundup was used when I first arrived to make a weed-free space for me to store potted plants and gardening equipment that I brought with me. This function has now been replaced in the following ways:
- lay down large sheets of thick carboard obtained from a whitegoods retailer
- lay down plastic and cover with several centimetres of dolomite sand
- use an organic herbicide
- use a flame weeder.

The second use is cut-and-swab or drill-and-fill to remove the stumps of very large mature trees that are too extensive or tangled for me to dig out.

At first I often start on a new area of tangled weeds thinking, 'This is pretty daunting, maybe I should use a herbicide', but I am always encouraged by my successes and keep going with manual control.

I rely more on hand-pulling than most other gardeners, perhaps because I am such an enthusiastic composter. I also use a trowel and taproot digger for bulbs and grasses, a mattock for blackberry and dock, secateurs and bush saws to pull ivy from trees and cut up woody weeds, and a mower to hold at bay big areas of grasses and three-corner garlic.

Gravel paths are flamed several times in spring to kill fog grass and keep Guildford grass suppressed. Guildford grass is almost gone, except for compacted surfaces such as driveways and paths.

Organic herbicide is used to control paths, weeds in summer — when it is too hot to flame — and to stop grasses from flowering on a steep embankment where I can't mulch and don't want to pull the weeds and damage the bank.

Index

A

Abutilon theophrasti, 129
Acacia, 9, 137, 138
  A. baileyana, 9
  A. nilotica, 13
  A. saligna, 9
  A. sophorae, 9
Acaena anserinifolia, 152
Achillea
  A. millefolium, 179, 208
  A. tomentosa, 72
African boxthorn. *see* boxthorn
African daisy, 1, 91, 186–7, 194, 221
African lovegrass, 162, 194
Agapanthus praecox, 183
Ageratum, 168
agricultural machinery, 6
Agropyron repens, 2, 162–3, 198
Agrostis stolonifera, 162, 198
Ailanthus altissima, 161
Ajuga reptans, 68
Alcea, 221
allelopathic plants, 53–4
alligator weed, 13
Allium ampeloprasum, 52
Allium triquetrum, 161, 206
Alocasia macrorrhiza, 52
Alternanthera
  A. philoxeroides, 13
  A. repens, 155
Alyssum, 56, 168, 211
amaranth, 26, 31
Amaranthus, 31
  A. retroflexus, 148
  A. viridis, 148, 200
Anagallis arvensis, 172, 204
Anemone, 221
animal manure (as mulch), 75
animals, use of, 130–2
Annona glabra, 13
annuals, 31–4, 144–51, 170–3
  grasses, 150–1
Apium graveolens, 52, 64
apple of Sodom, 123
aquatic weeds, 27, 183, 192
Arachis pintoi, 52
Arctotheca calendula, 14, 141, 146, 196
Artemisia absinthium, 54, 65
artichoke thistle, 152, 194
arugula. *see* rocket
arum lily, 183
Asparagus
  A. asparagoides, 13, 181, 187–8
  A. officinalis, 64
Asphodelus fistulosus, 156, 202

Athel pine, 13
Atriplex, 52
Austrodanthonia, 169
Austrostipa, 169
Avena, 53, 63, 150, 208
   A. barbata, 34
   A. fatua, 34
   A. sativa, 47

B

baby's tears, 57
bagasse (as mulch), 78
bamboo, 74, 174
Bambusa, 74, 174
banana passionfruit, 65
barley, 3, 7, 27, 47, 63
barleygrass, 27, 28, 150, 194
barnyard grass, 33, 150, 151
barrier planting, 64–6
basil, 52, 59, 164
Bathurst burr, 27, 134, 144–5, 194
beans, 48, 52, 62, 64, 84. *see also* broad beans
bearded oats, 34
beetles, as biological controls, 160
beetroot, 47, 48, 63, 84, 110
bellflower, 68
Bellis perennis, 2, 141, 177, 202
Beta vulgaris, 48, 63
bidgee-widgee, 152
biennials, 34, 151, 173–4
Billardiera heterophylla, 9
bindii, 88, 141, 145, 194

biodegradable films, 83
biodiversity, 167–8, 180–1
Biological Control Act 1985, 12
biological controls, 42, 50, 54, 129
   30, 134, 151, 154, 160, 187, 188,
   189, 190
bitou bush. *see* boneseed
black passionfruit, 65
black plastic technique, 124–8
blackberry, 13, 27, 40, 103, 104, 112,
   114, 123, 129, 131, 152, 181,
   184, 187, 194, 218, 219, 220, 222
blackberry nightshade, 27, 31, 151,
   160, 194, 221
bluebell creeper, 9
boneseed (bitou bush), 13, 138, 181,
   187, 194, 195
borage, 57, 170
Borago officinalis, 57, 170
boxthorn (African boxthorn), 27,
   138, 152
bracken, 27, 35, 132, 142, 152, 165,
   194
Bradley method, 183–4
Brassica, 10, 47, 48, 51, 59, 62, 63,
   64, 211
   B. oleracea, 63, 64
   B. rapa, 63
   B. rapa var. rapa, 64
briar rose, 138
bridal creeper, 13, 181, 187–8
bridal creeper leafhopper (insect),
   188
broad beans, 47, 52, 56, 62

broad-leaved dock, 154
broadleaf weeds, 18, 31, 88, 111, 122, 135, 136, 142, 143, 220
broadleafed plantain, 177
broccoli, 46, 48, 64, 75, 93, 211
broom, 22, 119, 138, 142, 219
brush-cutters, 113
buckwheat, 63
buffalo grass, 124, 125
bugle, 68
bulb diggers. *see* taproot diggers
bulb exhaustion, 94, 95, 156–7
burdock, 27
burgan, 9
bushland weed control, 139, 167, 183–5
buttercup, 17, 89, 141, 145–6, 196
button everlasting daisy, 168
button squash. *see* squash

C

cabbage, 48, 51, 63, 64, 147, 170, 211
Cabomba, 13, 192, 196
  C. caroliniana, 13, 192, 196
Cacatua tenuirostris (bird), 156
Cactoblastis moth, 129
California thistle, 27, 152–3
caltrop, 27, 33, 135, 146, 196
Campanula, 68, 221
camphor laurel, 137, 153, 181
Canada thistle (creeping thistle), 39, 153
Canadian fleabane, 147

Canna, 64, 163
Cape broom, 181, 188, 196
Cape lily, 1
Cape tulip, 1, 27, 123, 153–4, 181
Capeweed (South African capeweed), 14, 27, 28, 56, 88, 141, 142, 146, 196
Capsella bursa-pastoris, 31, 170, 172, 204
capsicum, 151
Cardamine hirsuta, 170, 198
carpet (as mulch), 83–4
Carpobrotus, 72
carrots, 47, 48, 50, 64, 85, 110, 120, 130, 131, 174
Carson, Rachel, 10
Carthamus lanatus, 131, 149, 204
case study (Tim's garden - Stirling), 88, 218–23
Cassia obtusifolia, 129
castor oil plant, 153
catnip, 68
cat's ear, 57, 141, 174, 196
cauliflower, 46, 63, 64
celery, 52, 64, 84
Centella asiatica, 58
Cerastium glomeratum, 141
cereal rye, 53, 63
Chamaesphecia doryliformis (moth), 154
charlock, 14, 147
chemical safety, 21–24
Chenopodium album, 14–5, 31, 53, 90, 171, 198

chickweed, 32, 50, 86, 89, 166, 170, 196, 220
chicory, 14, 175, 196
Chilean needle grass, 13
Chondrilla juncea, 160–1, 206
Chrysanthemoides monilifera, 13, 181, 187, 194
Chrysanthemum parthenium, 68
Chrysolina
  C. hyperici (beetle), 160
  C. quadrigemina (beetle), 160
Cichorium, 14, 196
Cinnamomum camphora, 137, 153, 181
Cirsium
  C. arvense, 39, 153
  C. californicum, 152–3
Cistus, 72
classification, of plants, 30–1
cleavers, 27, 89, 90, 146–7, 166, 196, 220
Clematis microphylla, 188
clever clover, 51–2
clover (trefoil), 7, 47, 50, 51–2, 53, 61, 62, 89, 140, 146, 166, 220, 221. *see also* red clover; strawberry clover; subterranean clover; sweet clover; white clover
clubroot, 14
coast tea tree, 9
coastal galenia, 174
coastal wattle, 9
Coleman, Eliot, 109

Coleman hoes, 109–10
Colletotrichum orbiculare, 134
comfrey, 64–5, 163
common horsetail, 39
compost, 77, 82, 96
controlled burning, 122–3
Convolvulus, 27
  C. arvensis, 154
Conyza, 198
  C. bonariensis, 147
Cootamundra wattle, 9
Coreopsis, 221
cork elm, 24, 138, 218
corn. *see* sweet corn
Correa decumbens, 68
Corsican mint, 57
Cortaderia selloana, 159, 184, 202
Corylus, 65
cotoneaster, 22, 137, 138, 218
couch grass, 2, 27, 35, 39, 64, 74, 76, 82, 96, 124, 125, 162–3, 198
cover crops, 50–9
  definition, 59
  examples, 56–9
cowpea, 62, 63
Crataegus, 138
  C. laevigata, 181
creeping bent grass, 162, 198
creeping boobialla, 68
creeping oxalis, 141, 156
creeping thistle. *see* Canada thistle
cress, 50, 170–1, 198
crimped rollers, 117–8

crop rotation, 7, 47–8
cross-grazing, 132
cruciferous weeds, 13–14, 147
Cryptostegia grandiflora, 13
cumbungi, 86
Curcubita, 52
Curcumis, 62
Cuscuta, 24
cut-and-swab technique, 22, 24, 138–9, 222
Cydonia oblonga, 65
Cynara
  C. cardunculus, 152, 194
  C. scolymus, 64
Cynodon dactylon, 124
Cyperus, 86
  C. rotundus, 35, 39, 141, 155–6, 202
Cytisus scoparius, 188, 198

D

daisy, 27, 148, 168, 170, 173. *see also* lawn daisy
daisy diggers. *see* taproot diggers
dandelion, 17, 26, 27, 34, 57–8, 91, 139, 141, 146, 166, 169, 172, 173, 174–6, 198, 220
darnel, 2
Datura, 28
  D. stramonium, 28, 149
Daucus carota, 48, 64, 174
Delphinium, 221
Dianthus, 72
Digitaria sanguinalis, 150, 206

Dioscorea, 52
diversity, 55
dock, 14, 26, 27, 28, 35, 89, 102, 141, 154, 165, 167, 198, 222
dock diggers, 102, 154
dock moth, 154
dodder, 4, 25
Dolichos, 63
double digging, 98–9
drainage, 86
draw hoes, 105–6
drill-and-fill. *see* cut-and-swab technique
drop-shank trowels, 101
Duncan, Dave, 93
Dutch clover. *see* white clover
Dutch hoes, 106
dyeweed, 2

E

Echinochloa
  E. crus-galli, 33, 150
  E. esculenta, 61, 63
Echium, 31, 170
  E. plantagineum, 1, 31, 151, 170, 202
ecological control programs, 15–16
ecology, 13–15
economic impact, 9–10
eggplant, 151
Eichhornia crassipes, 14, 86, 192, 208
Eleocharis dulcis, 86
Emex australis, 149

endive, 175
English broom, 123, 188, 198, 218
English ivy, 70
Environment Protection and Biodiversity Conservation Act 1999, 12
environmental weeds, 12, 65, 93, 180–192
　dumping garden waste, 181–3
　examples, 181, 186–192
ephemerals, 31
Equisetum, 74
　E. arvense, 39
Eragrostis curvula, 162, 194
Erica, 181, 189, 218
Erigeron, 198
　E. canadensis, 147
　E. elatior, 147
Eriobotrya japonica, 65
Eruca versicaria, 58
etiolated growth, 126–7
Euphorbia, 31, 149, 153
　E. peplus, 32, 149, 204
Exapion ulicis (weevil), 189

F

faba beans, see: broad beans
Fagopyrum esculentum, 63
false dandelion. *see* cat's ear
false seedbed. *see* stale seedbed
fan flower, 68, 168
fat hen, 14–5, 31, 53, 90, 165, 166, 171, 198
fava beans, see: broad beans

feather grass, 163, 198
feather top. *see* feather grass
fennel, 151
Festuca rubra, 162
feverfew, 68
field bindweed, 154
field peas. *see* peas
fishbone fern, 154
flame weeders, 121, 143
flat-leaf parsley, 63
flax leaf fleabane, 147
fleabane (horseweed), 56, 147–8, 198
Foeniculum vulgare, 151
forget-me-not, 171, 198, 221
fountain grass, 163, 181
Fumaria, 32, 89, 90, 171, 198
fumitory, 28, 32, 89, 90, 166, 171, 198, 220
fungi, 129, 134, 148
furse. *see* gorse

G

Galenia pubescens, 174
Galium
　G. aparine, 89, 90, 146–7, 196
　G. tricornutum, 147
garden cress, 50, 170
garden escapees. *see* garden weeds
garden forks, 102
garden heliotrope. *see* Valeriana officinalis (garden heliotrope)
garden weeds, 144–64, 173, 181–3
garlic, 84, 99, 164

Gazania, 70, 112, 183
genetically modified (GM) plants, 25
Genista, 123
  G. monspessulana, 181, 188, 196
geo-fabrics, 83
Geranium, 70
Gladiolus, 218
globe artichoke, 64
Glycine max, 63
glyphosate, 18–19, 136
GM plants. *see* genetically modified (GM) plants
goats, 131
golden wreath, 9
good weeds, 147, 169–179
goosefoot. *see* cleavers
goosegrass. *see* cleavers
gorse, 13, 22, 112, 123, 138, 154, 181, 189, 200
gorse seed weevil, 189
gorse spider mite, 189
gorse thrips, 189
Gotukola, 58
grass clippings (as mulch), 76–7, 82
green amaranth, 148, 200
green manure, 55–6, 59–63
  definition, 59
  examples, 62–3
Grevillea, 70
  G. rosmarinifolia, 9
groundcovers, 66–73, 168–9
  characteristics, 66–7
  examples, 68–73

groundsel, 31, 148, 200
guava, 65
Guildford grass, 89, 154–5, 200, 218, 219, 223
guinea pigs, 130–1
Gundaroo tiller, 103

H

hairy cress, 170, 198
hairy vetch, 56
hand forks, 101
hand pulling. *see* hand-weeding
hand tools, 100–10
hand trowels, 100–1
hand-weeding, 89–94, 97
hawthorn, 138, 181, 218
hazelnuts, 65
Heavy Cut mower, 113–5
hebe, 218
Hedera, 70
  H. Helix, 70
Helianthus tuberosus, 64, 169–70
Helichrysum scorpioides, 168
herbicides, 15. *see also* organic herbicides
  effectiveness, 19–20
  harm done by, 20–24
  history, 18–19
Ho-Mi (hoe), 109
hoeing, 98, 105, 110
hoes, 104–6
hogweed. *see* wireweed
holly, 22, 138

hollyhock, 221
Homeria, 1, 123, 181
　H. breyniana, 153-4
　H. miniata, 153-4
Hordeum
　H. glaucum, 150, 194
　H. vulgare, 47, 63
horehound, 155, 200
horsetail, 39, 74, 167
horseweed. *see* fleabane
Hybridisation, 25
Hydrocotyl umbellate, 86
Hymenachne, 13
　H. amplexicaulis, 13
Hypericum perforatum, 14, 132, 161, 206
Hypochaeris radicata, 57, 141, 174, 196

I

indigenous plants, 8-9
insects, 55-6
　beneficial, 2, 50, 52, 54, 55, 56, 57, 59, 89, 115, 167-8, 170, 173, 174, 175, 179
　as pests, 55-6
intercropping, 64
introduced plants, 7-8
Ipomoea
　I. batatas, 52, 63
　I. indica, 155, 184, 200
iris, 35, 40, 64, 212, 218
Isatis tinctoria, 2
ivy, 70, 164, 218, 222

J

Japanese millet, 61, 63
Jellybean plant, 72
Jerusalem artichoke, 64, 169-70
jo-jo. *see* bindii
Johnson grass, 117, 163, 200
Juncus, 86
Juniperus (juniper)
　J. communis, 70
　J. horizontalis, 70

K

kale, 48, 63
kama, 112
kangaroo grass, 169
Kennedia prostrata, 168
khaki weed, 155
kikuyu, 39, 74, 124, 125
Kniphofia uvaria, 163
Kunzea ericoides, 9

L

Lactuca
　L. sativa, 53
　L. serriola, 173, 204
lambs ear, 70
lambsquarters. *see* fat hen
Lantana, 13, 123, 184, 189-90, 200
　L. camara, 7, 13, 189-90, 200
lawn daisy, 2, 141, 177, 202
lawn weeds, 139-41
leaf-to-area index, 46, 51
leaves (as mulch), 76

leeks, 52, 65, 84, 122
legislation, 11–12
legumes, 48, 52, 60, 62, 63, 89, 166, 167
Lepidium sativum, 50, 170
Leptospermum laevigatum, 9
lesser periwinkle, 160, 202
lettuce, 28, 47, 53, 64, 93
lettuce necrotic yellows virus (LNYV), 13, 28
Ligustrum lucidum, 160, 184, 204
Lily, 35, 218, 219–20
liquid fertiliser, 65, 96
Listrodere (insect), 56
livestock, toxicity to, 14, 132, 147, 149, 150, 152, 174, 190, 209
LNYV. *see* lettuce necrotic yellows virus
Lobularia maritima, 56
Lolium, 2, 63, 150, 204
　L. perenne, 163
　L. temulentum, 2
long-billed corella, 156
loquat, 65
lucerne, 44, 62, 77
lupin, 62
Lupinus, 62
Lycium ferocissimum, 138, 152
Lycopersicon esculentum, 52

M

mallow, 148, 200
Malvia, 148, 200
Marrubium vulgare, 155, 200
marshmallow, 56
Matthiola incana, 221
mattocks, 103
MCPA (herbicide), 18
Medicago, 50
　M. sativa, 62
medics, 50, 52
melon, 62
Mentha
　M. pulegium, 14, 58, 172, 202
　M. requienii, 57
mesquite, 13
milfoil. *see* yarrow
milk thistle. *see* sow thistle
millet, 63
Mimosa, 13, 190
　M. pigra, 13, 190
minerals (as mulch), 79
mistletoe, 27
mites, 189
mixed cropping. *see* polyculture (mixed cropping)
morning glory, 155, 184, 200
mouse-ear chickweed, 141
mowing, 111–7
　techniques, 115–7
Mucuna pruriens, 52
Muehlenbeckia, 188
mulch, 74–82, 83, 85
　advantages, 79–80
　disadvantages, 80–2
　types, 75–9
mullein, 164, 221

mushroom compost (as mulch), 78
mustard, 47, 54, 63, 64, 211
Mycoherbicides, 129
Myoporum parvifolium, 68
Myosotis arvensis, 171, 198

N

narrow-leaf plantain, 177
Nassella
  N. neesiana, 13
  N. trichotoma, 13, 131
nasturtium, 64, 171–2
National Weeds Strategy 1998, 12
native grasses, 169
native plants, 8–9
native violet, 72
neem, 164
Nepeta faassenii, 68
Nephrolepis cordifolia, 154
nettle soup, 178
nettles. *see* stinging nettle
New Zealand spinach (Warrigal greens), 58
Nicotiana glauca, 15, 87
Noogoora burr, 148, 202
Norfolk system, 7
NRG Pro Weeder, 103
nutgrass, 35, 39, 79, 141, 155–6, 202
nutsedge. *see* nutgrass

O

oats, 47, 53, 63. *see also* bearded oats; wild oats

Ocimum basilicum, 52
Oenanthe pimpinelloides, 174
old man's beard, 188
Olea europaea, 65, 181
olives, 65, 181, 218
one-leaf Cape tulip, 153–4
onion grass. *see* Guildford grass
onion hoes, 106
onion weed, 156, 202
onions, 19, 40, 47, 84, 99, 110, 122
Opuntia, 7, 129, 160, 204
organic herbicides, 132–7, 143
Ornithogalum thyrsoides, 1
oscillating hoes. *see* stirrup hoes
Oxalis, 17, 49, 79, 88, 102, 156–9, 219–20
  O. corniculata, 141, 156
  O. corymbosa, 156
  O. perennans, 156
  O. pes-caprae, 1, 7, 93–7, 98, 156, 206
Ozothamnus, 168

P

pampas grass, 159, 184, 202
paper (as mulch), 75–6
Parkinsonia, 13
parsley, 85, 93, 94. *see also* flat-leaf parsley
parsnip, 48
Parthenium hysterophorus, 13
Paspalum, 117, 163, 202
  P. dilatatum, 163, 202

Passiflora
  P. edulis, 65
  P. millissima, 65
passionfruit. *see* banana passionfruit; black passionfruit
Pastinaca sativa, 48
pasture weeds, 142–3
Paterson's curse. *see* salvation Jane
pearlwort, 86, 141, 148–9, 202
peas (field peas), 44, 48, 56, 62
Pelargonium, 170, 221
  P. peltatum, 70
Pennisetum
  P. clandestinum, 124
  P. setaceum, 163, 181
  P. villosum, 163, 198
pennyroyal, 14, 58, 172, 202
pennywort, 86
perennial ryegrass, 163
perennials, 35–7, 151–163, 174–9
  control, 36–7
  grasses, 162–3
periwinkle, 136, 160, 202
Petroselenium crispum var. neapolitanum, 63
petty spurge, 32, 149, 204
Phaseolus, 48, 52
  P. vulgaris, 64
Phlox, 70
  P. subulata, 70
Phragmites communis, 86
pigface, 72, 168
pigs, 132

pigweed. *see* purslane
Pimelea, 168
  P. prostrata, 168
pine, 218
pink-flowered oxalis, 156
pinks, 72
pinto peanut, 52
Pinus radiata, 137
Pisum sativum, 48, 62
Pittosporum undulatum, 9, 181, 206
Plantago, 14, 90, 176–7, 204
  P. lanceolata, 141, 177
  P. major, 141, 177
plantain (ribwort), 14, 90, 141, 176–7, 204, 220. *see also* broadleafed plantain; narrow-leaf plantain
planting methods, 49–51
plums, 65, 218
Poa, 63, 117, 169
  P. annua, 31, 32, 151, 208
polyculture (mixed cropping), 52
Polygala myrtifolia var. myrtifolia, 181
Polygonum aviculare, 89, 150, 208
pond apple, 13
Portulaca oleracea, 33, 50, 90, 168, 172, 204
potato, 40, 48, 63, 95, 151, 178, 213
poultry, 130
prickly acacia, 13
prickly lettuce, 173, 204, 220
prickly pear, 7, 129, 160, 204
prickly sida, 129

privet, 160, 184, 204
proclaimed weeds, 11–12, 181
Prosopis species, 13
prostrate clover, 50
prostrate saltbush, 52
Prunus, 65
Psidium, 65
Pteridium esculentum, 152, 194
Puccinia
   P. chondrillina (rust fungus), 129
   P. myrsiphylli (rust fungus), 188
pumpkin, 93
purple nutgrass. *see* nutgrass
purple nutsedge. *see* nutgrass
purslane (pigweed), 33, 50, 90, 168, 169, 172, 204
push hoes, 106

Q
Quarantine Act 1908, 12
quassia, 164
Queen Anne's lace, 174
quince, 65

R
rabbits, 130–1
radiata pine, 137
radish, 63, 64, 211
ragwort, 132, 160, 204
raised beds, 49
rake-hoes, 104
rakes, 103–4
Ranunculus repens, 89, 141, 145–6, 196
Raphanus
   R. raphanistrum, 14, 147, 150, 208
   R. sativus, 63
Rapistrum rugosum, 14, 147, 206
raspberry, 219
red clover, 52
red fescue, 162
red-hot poker, 163
redroot amaranth, 148
reeds, 86
rhizomes, 125–6
rhus tree, 160
ribwort. *see* plantain
rice flower, 168
Ricinus communis, 153
rock rose, 72
rocket, 58, 64, 65, 93, 175
roguing, 28
Romulea rosea, 89, 154–5, 200
Rosa rubiginosa, 138
rosemary, 54, 72, 164
Rosmarinus officinalis, 54, 72
rotary hoes (rotovators), 111
rotenone, 164
rotovators. *see* rotary hoes
rubber vine, 13
Rubus, 181, 187
   R. fruticosus, 13, 152, 187, 194
rue, 164
Rumex, 14, 89, 141, 154, 198
   R. acetosella, 161, 206
   R. obtusifolius, 154
running postman, 168

rushes, 86
rust fungus, 129, 148, 161, 188
ryegrass, 2, 7, 56, 62, 63, 150, 204. *see also* perennial ryegrass

S

saffron thistle, 131, 149, 204
Sagina procumbens, 86, 141, 148-9, 202
Salix, 13
  S.babylonica, 13
  S.x calodendron, 13
  S.x reichardtii, 13
salvation Jane, 14, 27, 31, 112-13, 120, 129, 132, 151, 170, 202, 221
Salvinia, 13, 129, 192
  S. molesta, 13, 192
Scaevola
  S. aemula, 68
  S. albida, 68
scarlet pimpernel, 172, 204
Schomburgh, Richard, 156
scuffle hoes, 107-8
seaweed (as mulch), 78
Secale cereale, 53, 63
sedge, 35, 86, 155-6
Sedum, 72
  S. rubrotinctum, 72
  S. spectabile, 72
seed dormancy, 38-9
Senecio, 31, 200
  S. jacobaea, 132, 160, 204
  S. pterophorus, 1, 186-7, 194
  S. vulgaris, 148

Sericothrips staphylinus, 189
serrated tussock, 13, 131
sexual reproduction, 37-9
Shakespeare, 5
sheep, 131-2
shepherd's purse, 26-7, 28, 31, 170, 172, 204
shovels, 102
shredders, 111
sickle, 112
sicklepod, 129
Sida spinosa, 129
silver beet, 63
silver-leaf nightshade, 27, 160, 204
Silybum marianum, 131, 150, 208
Sinapis arvensis, 14, 147
Singapore daisy, 116
skeleton weed, 27, 129, 160-1, 206
slashing, 111-5, 142
slugs, 163-4
smother crop, 63-4
  definition, 63
snails, 163-4
soil condition, 14-15, 87, 165, 166-7
Solanum, 151
  S. elaeagnifolium, 160, 204
  S. hermanni, 123
  S. nigrum, 31, 151, 194
  S. tuberosum, 48, 63
solarisation, 123-4
Soleirolia soleirolii, 57
Soliva sessilis, 141, 145, 194

Sollya heterophylla. *see* Billardiera heterophylla
Sonchus oleraceus, 90, 172–3, 206
Sorghum, 53, 61
  S. bicolor drummondi, 63
  S. halepense, 117, 163, 200
sorrel, 27, 161, 165, 166, 206
soursob, 1, 7, 28, 98, 206, 218
  control, 93–7, 156–9
South African capeweed. *see* Capeweed
southernwood, 164
sow thistle (milk thistle), 90, 165, 166, 172–3, 206, 220, 221
soybean, 63
spades, 102
spading machines, 111
spear grass, 27, 169
Sphagneticola trilobata, 116
spin tillers (star hoes), 103, 109
spinach, 47, 51, 63, 64, 131, 171
Spinacia oleracea, 63, 64
spiny emex. *see* three-cornered Jack
spotted thistle. *see* variegated thistle
spreading correa, 68
spurge, 31, 149, 153, 167. *see also* petty spurge
squash, 52, 62, 75, 84
St John's wort, 14, 27, 132, 161, 206
Stachys byzantina, 70
stale seedbed, 50, 99–100
star hoes. *see* spin tillers
Stellaria media, 32, 50, 89, 170, 196

Stenotaphrum secundatum, 124
stinging nettle (nettles), 58, 89, 165, 166, 173, 177–9, 206
stinking roger, 58
stirrup hoes (oscillating hoes), 106–7
Stirzaker, Richard, 51
stock (animals), 142–3, 221
stolons, 125
stonecrop, 72
straw (as mulch), 77–8
strawberry clover, 52
Sturt's desert pea, 168
subterranean clover, 53
succulents, 37
Sudan grass, 53, 63
sumac. *see* rhus tree
summer grass, 150, 206
Swainsona formosa, 168
Swainsonia, 168
sweet clover, 56
sweet corn, 48, 52, 62, 84
sweet pittosporum, 9, 181, 206
sweet potato, 52, 63
Symphytum officinale, 64–5, 163

T

2,4-D (herbicide), 18
Tagetes minuta, 58
tall fleabane, 147
Tamarix aphylla, 13
taproot diggers (bulb diggers / daisy diggers), 101–2

Taraxacum officinale, 57–8, 141, 174–6, 198
taro, 52
temporary flooding, 86
Tetragonia tetragonoides, 58
Tetranychus lintearius (mite), 189
Themeda triandra, 169
thermal control, 119–124
thistle, 13, 26, 27, 28, 44, 56, 142. *see also* California thistle
thorn apple, 149
three-cornered garlic, 161, 206, 218, 220, 222
three-cornered Jack, 27, 149
three-horned bedstraw, 147
three-prong hoes, 108
thrips, 189
thyme, 58, 72
Thymus, 72
tobacco tree, 15, 87
tomato, 52, 59, 93, 151, 170
Toxicodendron succedaneum, 160
Tradescantia, 40
  T. albiflora, 116, 162, 184, 208
tree-of-heaven, 161
trefoil. *see* clover
Tribulus terrestris, 33, 135, 146, 196
Trifolium, 47, 62
  T. repens, 62, 179
Triticum, 63
Tropaeolum majus, 171
Tull, Jethro, 4, 6–7, 11
turnip, 7, 63, 64. *see also* wild turnip
turnip weed, 14, 147, 206
two-leaf Cape tulip, 153–4
tworks, 102–3
Typha, 86

U

U Bar, 103
Ulex europaeus, 13, 123, 154, 181, 189, 200
Ulmus thomasii, 24
undersowing, 50
unsightliness, 17–18
Urtica
  U. dioica, 173, 177, 206
  U. urens, 58, 89, 173, 206
useful weeds. *see* good weeds

V

Valeriana officinalis (garden heliotrope), 173, 208, 221
variegated thistle (spotted thistle), 131, 150, 208
vegetable weevil, 56
vegetative reproduction, 39–40
velvet bean, 52
velvetleaf, 129
Verbascum thapsus, 221
vetch, 47, 48, 63, 89, 94, 166
Vicia, 48
  V. faba, 47, 62
  V. villosa, 47, 63
Vigna, 48, 52
  V. unguiculata, 62, 63

Vinca
  V. major, 160, 202
  V. minor, 160, 202
Viola (violet)
  V. banksii, 179
  V. hederacea, 72, 179

W

wallaby grass, 169
wandering Jew, 40, 116, 162, 184, 208
warren hoes, 108
Warrigal greens. *see* New Zealand spinach
water chestnuts, 86
water dropwort, 174
water hyacinth, 14, 27, 86, 192, 208
water restriction, 85–6
water weeds. *see* aquatic weeds
Watsonia, 35, 40, 96, 102–3, 123, 181, 190–2, 211, 218
wattle, 9, 24. *see also* coastal wattle; Cootamundra wattle; golden wreath
weed control, 15–17, 19–20, 59, 139, 183–4, 193–209. *see also* biological controls; bushland weed control; thermal control
  barriers, 74, 83–4, 163
  black plastic technique, 124–8
  controlled burning, 122–3
  cultivation, 98
  cutting, 137
  grazing animals, 130–2
  hand-pulling, 89–94, 97
  hot water, 122, 142
  light restriction, 44–5
  mechanical tools, 138
  naked flame, 119–122, 142
  nutrient manipulation, 86–7, 88–9
  organic control, 42–3, 50–1
  quarantine and hygiene, 43–5
  ringbarking, 137–8
  steam, 122
  tree-poppers, 138
  water management, 85–6
weed management, 11–12, 87, 118–9
weed-proof fabrics, 83–4
weed replacement therapy, 93
weeds
  benefits, 14–15, 165–7
  characteristics, 29–30
  definition, 1–3
  history, 3–4
  indicators of soil type, 89, 165
  language and literature, 4–5
  as mulch, 79
  negative effects, 14–15, 24–5
  spread, 26–8, 37–8
  transporting, 118
Weeds of National Significance (WONS), 12–13, 187, 188, 189, 190, 192
weevils, 56, 129.189
weod, 2
wheat, 7, 63, 156

wheel hoes, 108
whipper snippers, 113
white clover, 52, 53, 62, 179, 220
White flowering sweet alyssum. *see* Alyssum
white hellebore, 164
wild garlic, 14
wild lettuce. *see* prickly lettuce
wild oats, 34, 150, 208
wild radish, 14, 147, 150, 208
wild turnip, 28
willow, 13
winter grass, 31, 32, 151, 208
winter rye, 53
wireweed (hogweed), 89, 150, 208
woad, 2
WONS. *see* Weeds of National Significance (WONS)
woody weeds, 22, 24, 137–9, 185, 222
woody yarrow, 72
wormwood, 54, 65, 164

X

Xanthium
X. occidentale, 134, 144–5, 148, 194, 202

Y

yam, 52
yarrow, 167, 179, 208

Z

Zantedeschia aethiopica, 183
Zea mays, 48, 52
zucchini, 51, 75, 131
Zyginia (insect), 188

www.ingramcontent.com/pod-product-compliance
Lightning Source LLC
Chambersburg PA
CBHW022047290426
44109CB00014B/1017